Congressional
Research
Service

EPA Regulations:
Too Much, Too Little, or On Track?

James E. McCarthy
Specialist in Environmental Policy

Claudia Copeland
Specialist in Resources and Environmental Policy

April 25, 2012

Congressional Research Service

7-5700

www.crs.gov

R41561

Summary

Since Barack Obama was sworn in as President in 2009, the Environmental Protection Agency (EPA) has proposed and promulgated numerous regulations implementing the pollution control statutes enacted by Congress. Critics have reacted strongly. Many, both within Congress and outside of it, have accused the agency of reaching beyond the authority given it by Congress and ignoring or underestimating the costs and economic impacts of proposed and promulgated rules. The House has conducted vigorous oversight of the agency in the 112th Congress, and has approved several bills that would overturn specific regulations or limit the agency's authority. Particular attention is being paid to the Clean Air Act, under which EPA has moved forward with the first federal controls on emissions of greenhouse gases and also addressed emissions of conventional pollutants from a number of industries.

Environmental groups disagree that the agency has overreached, and EPA states that critics' focus on the cost of controls obscures the benefits of new regulations, which, it estimates, far exceed the costs; and it maintains that pollution control is an important source of economic activity, exports, and American jobs. Further, the agency and its supporters say that EPA is carrying out the mandates detailed by Congress in the federal environmental statutes.

This report provides background information on recent EPA regulatory activity to help address these issues. It examines 40 major or controversial regulatory actions taken by or under development at EPA since January 2009, providing details on the regulatory action itself, presenting an estimated timeline for completion of the rule (including identification of related court or statutory deadlines), and, in general, providing EPA's estimates of costs and benefits, where available. The report includes tables that show which rules have been finalized and which remain under development.

The report also discusses factors that affect the timeframe in which regulations take effect, including statutory and judicial deadlines, public comment periods, judicial review, and permitting procedures, the net results of which are that existing facilities are likely to have several years before being required to comply with most of the regulatory actions under discussion. Unable to account for such factors, which will vary from case to case, timelines that show dates for proposal and promulgation of EPA standards effectively underestimate the complexities of the regulatory process and overstate the near-term impact of many of the regulatory actions.

Contents

Tables

Contacts

Introduction

Is EPA on Target or Overreaching? Conflicting Views

Since Barack Obama was sworn in as President of the United States in 2009, the Environmental Protection Agency (EPA) has proposed and promulgated numerous regulations under the 11 pollution control statutes Congress has directed it to implement.[1] Most of these statutes have not been amended for more than a decade, yet the agency is still addressing for the first time numerous directives given it by Congress, while also addressing newly emerging pollution problems and issues. The statutes also mandate that EPA conduct periodic reviews of many of the standards it issues, and the agency is doing these reviews, as well.

Although supporters would say that EPA is just doing its job, the agency's recent regulatory actions have drawn attention for several reasons. In some cases, such as regulation of greenhouse gas emissions, they represent a new departure. Based on a 2007 Supreme Court ruling that greenhouse gas emissions are air pollutants under the Clean Air Act's definition of that term,[2] the agency has undertaken numerous regulatory actions setting emission standards or laying the framework for a future regulatory structure. In other cases, the agency is revisiting emissions, effluent, and waste management regulatory decisions made during earlier Administrations and proposing more stringent standards to address pollution that persists as long as 40 years after Congress directed the agency to take action. These actions are being driven by statutory requirements to reexamine regulations, by court decisions, or because of changing technologies or new scientific information.

EPA's actions, both individually and in sum, have generated controversy. *The Wall Street Journal*, calling the current scale of EPA regulatory actions "unprecedented," has stated that the agency "has turned a regulatory firehose on U.S. business"[3] and, regarding proposed regulatory actions affecting electric generating units, it has said "the EPA's regulatory cascade is a clear and present danger to the reliability and stability of the U.S. power system and grid."[4] The American Enterprise Institute has stated that EPA "is engaged in a series of rule-making proceedings of extraordinary scope and ambition."[5] Affected parties, such as the National Petrochemical & Refiners Association, have labeled the agency's actions "overreaching government regulation" and "a clear distortion of current environmental law,"[6] while the National Mining Association has said, "even at a time of great economic stress, EPA is poised to enact a series of back-door

---

[1] For a summary of each of the 11 statutes and their principal requirements, see CRS Report RL30798, *Environmental Laws Summaries of Major Statutes Administered by the Environmental Protection Agency*, coordinated by David M. Bearden.

[2] See CRS Report R40984, *Legal Consequences of EPA's Endangerment Finding for New Motor Vehicle Greenhouse Gas Emissions*, by Robert Meltz.

[3] *The Wall Street Journal*, "The EPA Permitorium," editorial, November 22, 2010.

[4] *The Wall Street Journal*, "An EPA Moratorium," editorial, August 29, 2011.

[5] AEI, "The EPA's Ambitious Regulatory Agenda," Conference, November 8, 2010, at http://www.aei.org/event/100334#doc.

[6] NPRA, "NPRA Says Court Decision on GHGs Bad for Consumers," December 10, 2010, at http://www.npra.org/newsRoom/?fa=viewCmsItem&title=Latest%20News&articleID=5980.

mandates that threaten to cost millions of American jobs, and increase the cost of their electricity while they're at it."[7]

Both Democrats and Republicans in Congress have expressed concerns, through bipartisan letters commenting on proposed regulations and through introduced legislation that would delay, limit, or prevent certain EPA actions.[8] Senior Republicans in the House and Senate have stated that they are committed to vigorous oversight of the agency's actions during the 112th Congress,[9] with some threatening to withhold funding if the agency continues on its present course.[10]

EPA Administrator Lisa Jackson has not been silent as the agency's actions have come under attack. In a November 2010 letter to the ranking Members of the Energy and Commerce Committee and its Subcommittee on Oversight and Investigations, she stated:

> The pace of EPA's Clean Air Act regulatory work under this administration is actually not faster than the pace under either of the two previous administrations. In fact, EPA has finalized or proposed fewer Clean Air Act rules (87) over the past 21 months than in the first two years of either President George W. Bush's administration (146) or President Clinton's administration (115).[11]

In congressional testimony and other fora, the Administrator has sought to rebut critics' challenges to EPA's actions and initiatives.

> It's time for a real conversation about protecting our health and the environment while growing our economy. EPA's 40 years of environmental and health protection demonstrate our nation's ability to create jobs while we clear our air, water and land.... Telling the truth about our economy and our environment is about respecting the priorities of the American people. More than 70 percent of Americans want EPA to continue to do its job effectively. Those same Americans want to see a robust economic recovery. We have the capacity to do both things if we don't let distractions keep us from the real work of creating jobs.[12]

---

[7] National Mining Association, "EPA's Regulatory Train Wreck," 2011, http://www.nma.org/pdf/fact_sheets/epa_tw.pdf.

[8] For a discussion of some of these congressional actions, see CRS Report R41212, *EPA Regulation of Greenhouse Gases Congressional Responses and Options*, by James E. McCarthy;CRS Report R41698, *H.R. 1 Full-Year FY2011 Continuing Resolution Overview of Environmental Protection Agency (EPA) Provisions*, by Robert Esworthy; and CRS Report R41979, *Environmental Protection Agency (EPA) FY2012 Appropriations Overview of Provisions in H.R. 2584 as Reported*, by Robert Esworthy.

[9] See, for example, Letter of Hon. Fred Upton, Chairman-elect, House Energy and Commerce Committee, and Hon. James Inhofe, Ranking Member, Senate Environment and Public Works Committee, to EPA Administrator Lisa Jackson, December 9, 2010, at http://epw.senate.gov/public/index.cfm?FuseAction=Files.View&FileStore_id=d596d5fb-593c-4c99-b0c1-41aab15887b0. See also "A Coming Assault on the E P.A.," *New York Times*, editorial, December 24, 2010.

[10] See letter of Hon. Jerry Lewis to EPA Administrator Lisa P. Jackson, November 29, 2010, p. 2, at http://op.bna.com/env.nsf/id/jstn-8bnt7t/.

[11] Letter of Lisa P. Jackson, EPA Administrator, to Hon. Joe Barton and Hon. Michael C. Burgess, November 8, 2010, p. 1. According to the letter, "All three counts include all Clean Air Act rules that amend the Code of Federal Regulations and that require the EPA Administrator's signature." Administrator Jackson's letter was written in response to an October 14 letter from Reps. Barton and Burgess in which they expressed concern regarding the cumulative impacts of new regulations being proposed under the Clean Air Act.

[12] Lisa P. Jackson, EPA Administrator, "Telling the Truth about the Environment and Our Economy," September 2, 2011, http://blog.epa.gov/administrator.

Environmental groups generally believe that the agency is moving in the right direction, but in several cases they would like the regulatory actions to be stronger.[13] Many also fear that recent decisions to delay the issuance or implementation of several standards are bad omens. Commenting on EPA's December 2010 request to delay the issuance of standards for boilers, Clean Air Watch stated, "there is an unfortunate appearance here that political pressure from Congress is affecting the situation. That EPA is running scared."[14] These concerns were renewed following the President's September 2011 decision to withdraw revised air quality standards for ozone that EPA had spent two years developing (see "Ambient Air Quality Standards" section, below).

It is not this report's purpose to render a verdict on whether EPA is overreaching, running scared, or following the directions and using the authorities given it by Congress. Statements characterizing EPA's actions, such as those cited above, depend on judgments as to whether the agency has correctly determined the level of stringency needed to address an environmental problem, and whether the agency's actions are justified by the legislative mandates that Congress has imposed. Congress and the courts may render these judgments.

What This Report Does

This report provides a factual basis for discussion of these issues, which must ultimately be evaluated on a case-by-case basis. The report identifies and briefly characterizes major regulatory actions[15] promulgated, proposed, or under development by EPA since January 2009. The report uses data from EPA's Spring 2011 Semiannual Regulatory Agenda[16] and the list of economically significant reviews conducted by the Office of Management and Budget (OMB)[17] to compile a list of 40 regulatory actions proposed, promulgated, or under development by the agency. The list includes all EPA rules considered "economically significant" by OMB since January 2009,[18] as well as some others that were not so designated but have been widely discussed.

Each entry in this report (1) gives the name or, where appropriate, the common name of the regulatory action (e.g., the "Tailoring Rule," or the "Endangerment Finding"); (2) explains what the action does; (3) states the current status of the rule or action (e.g., proposed July 6, 2010); (4) explains the significance of the action, often providing information on estimated costs and

---

[13] See, for example, comments of Clean Air Task Force, Earthjustice, Natural Resources Defense Council, and the Sierra Club on the proposed emission standards for boilers, as cited in CRS Report R41459, *EPA's Boiler MACT Controlling Emissions of Hazardous Air Pollutants*, by James E. McCarthy, p. 15.

[14] Clean Air Watch, "EPA Seeks Big Delay in Final Toxic Rule for Boilers," December 7, 2010, at http://blogforcleanair.blogspot.com/2010/12/epa-seeks-big-delay-in-final-toxic-rule.html.

[15] This report uses the terms "regulatory action," "regulation," "rule," "standard," and "guidelines" for the actions it describes. There are slight differences among these terms, which are explained, if necessary to understand how the regulatory action will be implemented. In general, "regulatory action" is the broadest of the terms and includes each of the others.

[16] U.S. EPA, *Semiannual Regulatory Agenda Spring 2011*, at http://www.regulations.gov/#!documentDetail;D=EPA-HQ-OA-2011-0592-0001

[17] OMB, Office of Information and Regulatory Affairs (OIRA), *Historical Reports* at http://www.reginfo.gov/public/do/eoHistReviewSearch.

[18] OIRA (the regulatory affairs staff within OMB) considers a rule to be "economically significant" if it is "likely to have an annual effect on the economy of $100 million or more or adversely affect in a material way the economy, a sector of the economy, productivity, competition, jobs, the environment, public health or safety, or State, local, or tribal governments or communities." OMB, *FAQs/Resources*, at http://www.reginfo.gov/public/jsp/Utilities/faq.jsp.

benefits; (5) discusses the timeline for implementation, and whether there is a non-discretionary congressional deadline or a court order or remand driving its development; and (6) identifies a CRS analyst who would be the contact for further information. To simplify presentation, in some cases, we have summarized several separate, but related, regulations under one heading.

This is not a complete list of the regulations that EPA has promulgated or proposed during the Obama Administration. Rather, it is an attempt to identify the most significant and most controversial. A complete list would be substantially longer.

A Few Caveats Regarding Timing

Not all of these rules are Obama Administration initiatives. Many began development under the Bush Administration, including several that were promulgated under that Administration and subsequently were vacated or remanded to EPA by the courts. Within the Clean Air Act group, for example, most of the major rules, including the agency's boiler rules and two of the major rules affecting electric power plants (the Cross-State Air Pollution Rule and the MACT rule) fit that description. Other EPA actions, such as reconsideration of the ozone air quality standard, have actually delayed for several years implementation of Bush Administration rules that would have strengthened existing standards. All of these are described in detail below.

Several other generalizations are worth underlining:

- Many proposed and "pre-proposal" rules linger for years without being promulgated; thus, many of the EPA actions described here may not take effect for some time.[19] For those rules not yet promulgated, we have focused on rules that have statutory or court-ordered deadlines and/or that have already been the subject of significant discussion.

- If there are no deadlines, we have attempted to provide EPA's estimate of the schedule for promulgation. In some cases, EPA has not estimated a promulgation date. In those instances, we have either provided dates reported in press accounts or we have discussed the general outlook for promulgation. Experience suggests that proposal or promulgation may take longer than estimated in cases that do not have a court-ordered deadline.

- Although they are the most likely deadlines to be met, even court-ordered dates for proposal or promulgation may change. It is not uncommon for EPA to request extensions of time, often due to the need to analyze extensive comments.

- Promulgation of standards is not the end of the road. Virtually all major EPA regulatory actions are subjected to court challenge, frequently delaying implementation for years. As noted earlier, many of the regulatory actions described here are the result of courts remanding and/or vacating rules promulgated by previous administrations.

- In many cases, EPA rules must be adopted by states to which the program has been delegated. Moreover, many states require that the legislature review new regulations before the new rules would take effect.

---

[19] They may also be substantially altered before they become final, as a result of the proposal and public comment process, and/or judicial review.

- Standards for stationary sources under the air, water, and solid waste laws are generally implemented through permits, which would be individually issued by state permitting authorities after the standards take effect. When finalized, a permit would generally include a compliance schedule, typically giving the permittee several years for installation of required control equipment. Existing sources generally will have several years following promulgation and effective dates of standards, therefore, to comply with any standards.

In short, the road to EPA regulation is rarely a straight path. There are numerous possible causes of delay. It would be unusual if the regulatory actions described here were all implemented on the anticipated schedule, and even if they were, existing facilities would often have several years before being required to comply. That said, **Table 1** identifies rules that are likely to be proposed or promulgated by the end of 2012.

Congressional Activity

In the 111th Congress, a number of EPA's regulatory actions were the subject of legislative proposals, including stand-alone bills that would have delayed or prohibited EPA actions, resolutions of disapproval under the Congressional Review Act, and potential riders on EPA's FY2010 appropriation. None of these measures passed.

In the 112th Congress, criticism of EPA actions has increased, and legislation to prevent or delay EPA action has passed the House. More legislation is considered likely. Some proposals are broad in nature, targeting EPA generally or a lengthy list of specifics, while others focus more narrowly on individual rules or actions.

The situation has been particularly contentious for regulatory actions involving greenhouse gases. Although Administrator Jackson and President Obama have repeatedly expressed their preference for Congress to take the lead in designing a GHG regulatory system, EPA maintains that, in the absence of congressional action, it must proceed to regulate GHG emissions using existing authority: a 2007 Supreme Court decision (*Massachusetts v. EPA*) compelled EPA to consider whether GHGs are air pollutants that endanger public health and welfare, and if it so determined, to embark on a regulatory course that is prescribed by the Clean Air Act. Having made an affirmative decision on the endangerment question, EPA is now proceeding on that regulatory course and is defending its actions in court.

Opponents of this effort in Congress, who maintain that the agency is exceeding its authority, have considered various approaches to altering the agency's course. For example, in February 2011, the House passed H.R. 1, a continuing resolution (CR) providing FY2011 full-year funding for EPA and other federal agencies and departments. As passed by the House, the bill contained more than 20 provisions restricting or prohibiting the use of appropriated funds to implement various regulatory activities under the EPA's jurisdiction—many of them focused on GHGs.[20] (On March 9, 2011, the Senate failed to approve the House-passed bill and subsequently also did not agree to a substitute text (S.Amdt. 149) that contained different funding levels and generally omitted the EPA regulatory provisions in the House-passed bill.)

---

[20] For information, see CRS Report R41698, *H.R. 1 Full-Year FY2011 Continuing Resolution Overview of Environmental Protection Agency (EPA) Provisions*, by Robert Esworthy.

The House also approved legislation to restrict EPA authority and to repeal a dozen EPA regulatory actions dealing with greenhouse gases (H.R. 910), on April 7, 2011. In the Senate, an amendment identical to H.R. 910 (S.Amdt. 183) failed on a vote of 50-50.

**Table 1. Major EPA Rules Expected to Be Proposed or Promulgated,
April-December 2012**

Item Number in this Report	Name of Rule	Type of Rule	Expected Date
30.	"Post-Construction" Stormwater Rule	Proposal	April
27.	Phase 2 Florida Numeric Nutrient Water Quality Standards	Proposal	May
11.	Particulate Matter (including "farm dust") NAAQS	Proposal	June
24.	Tier 3 Motor Vehicle Emission and Fuel Standards	Proposal	July
31.	Revised Cooling Water Intake Rule	Final	July
32.	Revised Steam Electric Effluent Guideline	Proposal	July
16, 17, 18, and 40.	Boiler MACT and related rules	Final	uncertain[a]
7.	GHG Emission Standards for Refineries	Proposal	uncertain
15.	Greenhouse Gas (GHG) Emission Standards for Power Plants	Final	uncertain[b]

Source: Compiled by CRS.

Notes: Expected dates are tentative.

a.   EPA projected promulgation of the boiler rules by the end of April 2012, but as of this writing, the rules had not gone to OMB for review.

b.   Under a consent agreement signed in December 2010, EPA was to promulgate this rule by May 26, 2012. The agency's schedule slipped by eight months before the rule was proposed. Thus, the final rule is likely to be delayed.

In reporting H.R. 2584, which would have provided EPA funding for FY2012, the House Appropriations Committee included more than 25 provisions intended to restrict or preclude the use of funds to proceed with recent or pending EPA regulatory actions.[21] These provisions were not included in the final appropriation, however (P.L. 112-74, enacted in December 2011).

---

[21] For information, see CRS Report R41979, *Environmental Protection Agency (EPA) FY2012 Appropriations Overview of Provisions in H.R. 2584 as Reported*, by Robert Esworthy.

Also in the 112th Congress, a number of bills addressing individual EPA regulations have been introduced and considered. In addition to H.R. 910, five of these bills (H.R. 1633, H.R. 2250, H.R. 2273, H.R. 2401, and H.R. 2681) have passed the House. The five bills would prevent, revoke, or direct EPA actions on rural dust, boilers and incinerators, coal combustion waste, electric power plants, and cement kilns, respectively. Resolutions of disapproval under the Congressional Review Act have also been introduced for specific EPA regulations. S.J.Res. 27, which would have struck EPA's Cross-State Air Pollution Rule, was rejected by the Senate in November 2011, but other resolutions may come to the floor.

Beyond the criticism of individual regulations, there also are calls for broad regulatory reforms, for example to reinforce the role of economic considerations in agency decision-making, to increase Congress's role in approving or disapproving regulatory decisions, or to require analysis of the cumulative impacts of multiple EPA regulations. One such broad bill is H.R. 10, the Regulations from the Executive in Need of Scrutiny (REINS) Act, which in general provides that major rules of the executive branch shall have no force or effect unless a joint resolution of approval is enacted into law.[22] The bill passed the House December 7, 2011. The House also passed H.R. 3010, the Regulatory Accountability Act,[23] and H.R. 527, the Regulatory Flexibility Improvements Act, in December. Among other provisions, the first of these bills would require agencies to adopt the least costly rule that meets relevant statutory objectives unless the benefits justify additional costs, provides for judicial review of certain requirements and determinations for which judicial review is not currently available, and impacts existing case law on judicial deference to agency interpretations of rules. The second bill, among other provisions, would requires agencies to provide the Chief Counsel of the Small Business Administration with all materials prepared or utilized in making a proposed rule and information on the potential adverse and beneficial economic impacts of the proposed rule on small entities, and it would require the Chief Counsel to convene a panel to review such materials.

Another broad bill, H.R. 2401, the Transparency in Regulatory Analysis of Impacts on the Nation (TRAIN) Act of 2011, passed the House in September 2011. Besides revoking regulations on electric power plants that EPA has promulgated, it would establish a panel of representatives of federal agencies to report to Congress on the cumulative economic impact of a number of listed EPA rules, guidelines, and actions concerning clean air and waste management, and it would require the EPA Administrator to take feasibility and costs into consideration in setting National Ambient Air Quality Standards, reversing a Supreme Court decision that found EPA could not consider costs in setting health-based ambient air quality standards. Among the motivations for the TRAIN Act is the widely expressed concern that when EPA analyzes impacts of individual regulations, it does not consider costs imposed by multiple rules taking effect more or less simultaneously.[24]

A number of other bills have been introduced in the House and Senate.

---

[22] For information, see CRS Report R41651, *REINS Act Number and Types of "Major Rules" in Recent Years*, by Maeve P. Carey and Curtis W. Copeland.

[23] For information, see CRS Report R42104, *An Overview and Analysis of H.R. 3010, the Regulatory Accountability Act of 2011*, by Vanessa K. Burrows and Maeve P. Carey.

[24] EPA analyses of the impact of new regulations generally construct a baseline of other state and federal regulations that have been promulgated and court decisions or consent agreements that have been finalized as of the date of a new regulation's proposal or promulgation. If other regulations under development at the same time are not yet final, the agency does not include the potential impact in its analysis, since regulations under development are often modified, delayed, or withdrawn before promulgation.

Organization of the Report

This report organizes the regulatory actions it describes under four headings: Clean Air Act and Climate Change; Clean Water Act; Toxic Substances Control Act; and Solid Waste (Resource Conservation and Recovery Act). A majority of the rules (25 of the 40) are being developed under the regulatory authority of the Clean Air Act. To help organize the presentation of these 25, we have grouped rules addressing specific issues (e.g., climate change, ambient air quality standards, etc.) together under subheadings. Following the text, the information is summarized in the form of two tables. **Table 2** shows which rules have been finalized, and **Table 3** shows rules which remain under development.

Clean Air Act and Climate Change

Climate Change

1. **Greenhouse Gas Reporting Rule.** On October 30, 2009, in response to a congressional mandate in EPA's FY2008 appropriation (P.L. 110-161), EPA promulgated the Greenhouse Gas Reporting Rule.[25] The rule required 31 categories of sources to report their emissions of greenhouse gases to EPA annually, beginning in 2011, if the sources emit 25,000 tons or more of carbon dioxide or the equivalent amount of five other greenhouse gases (GHGs).[26] (Eleven other categories of sources have since been added to the rule.) By itself, the rule imposes little cost ($867 per facility, according to EPA's estimate) because it only requires reporting; but the sources who are required to report are expected to be the focus of EPA efforts as the agency develops regulations to control emissions of GHGs. The original reporting deadline was March 31, 2011. As that date approached, EPA extended the deadline to September 30. The first data submitted under the rule were released January 11, 2012. For additional information, contact Jim McCarthy (7-7225, jmccarthy@crs.loc.gov).

2. **Greenhouse Gas Endangerment Finding.** On December 15, 2009, EPA issued findings that six greenhouse gases cause or contribute to air pollution that endangers public health and welfare.[27] The action was taken in response to an April 2007 Supreme Court decision (*Massachusetts v. EPA*) that required the agency to decide the issue or to conclude that climate change science is so uncertain as to preclude making such findings. These findings do not themselves impose any requirements on industry or other entities. However, the action was a prerequisite to finalizing EPA's greenhouse gas emission standards for cars and light duty trucks, which were jointly promulgated by EPA with fuel economy standards from the Department of Transportation, on May 7, 2010. These, in turn, triggered permit requirements for stationary sources of GHGs, beginning January 2, 2011. On December 10, 2010, the U.S. Court of Appeals

---

[25] U.S. Environmental Protection Agency, "Mandatory Reporting of Greenhouse Gases; Final Rule," 74 *Federal Register* 56260, October 30, 2009.

[26] GHG emissions consist of carbon dioxide (CO_2), methane, nitrous oxide (N_2O), sulfur hexafluoride (SF_6), and two categories of gases—hydrofluorocarbons (HFCs) and perfluorocarbons (PFCs). Since each of these substances has a different global warming potential, the emissions of each are converted to the equivalent amount of CO_2 emissions, based on how potent the substance is as compared to CO_2, giving rise to the term "CO_2-equivalent."

[27] U.S. Environmental Protection Agency, "Endangerment and Cause or Contribute Findings for Greenhouse Gases Under Section 202(a) of the Clean Air Act," 74 *Federal Register* 66496, December 15, 2009.

---

for the D.C. Circuit denied industry and state motions to stay the endangerment finding and related regulations. The court's order applied to 84 cases filed by a variety of industry groups and states (*Coalition for Responsible Regulation v. EPA*). For additional information, contact Jim McCarthy (7-7225, jmccarthy@crs.loc.gov).

3. **Light Duty Motor Vehicle Greenhouse Gas Rules.** On May 7, 2010, EPA and the National Highway Traffic Safety Administration (NHTSA) promulgated integrated GHG emission standards and corporate average fuel economy (CAFE) standards for new cars and light trucks, a category that includes SUVs and minivans, as well as pickup trucks.[28] NHTSA is required by the Energy Independence and Security Act of 2007 (EISA, P.L. 110-140) to promulgate CAFE standards so that by 2020, new cars and light trucks reach a combined average fuel economy of 35 miles per gallon (mpg). EPA simultaneously issued vehicle greenhouse gas standards in response to directives from the Supreme Court in *Massachusetts v. EPA*. The regulations require an increase in fuel economy to 34.1 mpg by model year 2016. The Administration estimates that complying with the regulations will add $1,100 to the cost of an average vehicle, although this additional purchase cost is expected to be paid back through lifetime fuel savings. The new standards are being phased in beginning with the 2012 model year. EPA estimates that the additional lifetime cost of 2012-2016 model year vehicles under the regulations will be about $52 billion; benefits are expected to be approximately $240 billion. EPA and NHTSA have also proposed joint GHG/fuel economy rules for 2017-2025 model year vehicles. On July 29, 2011, the White House announced that it had reached agreement with 13 auto manufacturers, the United Auto Workers, the state of California, and other interested parties under which GHG emissions from new cars and light trucks will be reduced about 50% by 2025, and average fuel economy will rise to nearly 50 miles per gallon. EPA and NHTSA formally proposed these standards on December 1, 2011.[29] The agencies estimate that the new technology to comply with the standards will cost roughly $2,000 per vehicle in 2025, although lifetime fuel savings will total roughly $5,000 to $6,000. For additional information, contact Brent Yacobucci (7-9662, byacobucci@crs.loc.gov).

4. **Greenhouse Gas Tailoring Rule.** On June 3, 2010, EPA promulgated a rule that defines which stationary sources will be required to obtain Clean Air Act permits for GHG emissions and how the requirements will be phased in.[30] The threshold set by the rule (annual emissions of 75,000-100,000 tons of carbon dioxide equivalents) will limit which facilities will be required to obtain permits: from 2011 through 2016, the nation's largest GHG emitters, including power plants, refineries, cement production facilities, and about two dozen other categories of sources (an estimated 17,000 facilities annually) will be the only sources required to obtain permits. Of these, most will face only an administrative requirement to provide an estimate of their GHG emissions, but EPA estimated that 1,600 new or modified facilities will need to address whether they have the best available control technology for limiting emissions.[31] Smaller businesses, almost all

---

[28] U.S. Environmental Protection Agency, U.S. Department of Transportation, "Light-Duty Vehicle Greenhouse Gas Emission Standards and Corporate Average Fuel Economy Standards; Final Rule," 75 *Federal Register* 25324-25728, May 7, 2010.

[29] EPA and NHTSA, "2017 and Later Model Year Light-Duty Vehicle Greenhouse Gas Emissions and Corporate Average Fuel Economy Standards; Proposed Rule," 76 *Federal Register* 74854-75420, December 1, 2011.

[30] U.S. Environmental Protection Agency, "Prevention of Significant Deterioration and Title V Greenhouse Gas Tailoring Rule; Final Rule," 75 *Federal Register* 31514, June 3, 2010.

[31] In the first 11 months of the program, however, EPA reports that only 68 permit applications were received. See U.S. EPA, Prevention of Significant Deterioration and Title V Greenhouse Gas Tailoring Rule Step 3, GHG Plantwide Applicability Limitations and GHG Synthetic Minor Limitations, Proposed Rule, 77 *Federal Register* 14233, March 8, (continued...)

farms, and large residential structures (about 6 million sources in all these categories), which would otherwise be required to obtain permits once GHGs became regulated pollutants under the act, are excluded by the rule's threshold limits and thus are shielded from permitting requirements by this rule. For additional information, contact Jim McCarthy (7-7225, jmccarthy@crs.loc.gov).

5. **PSD and Title V Permit Requirements for GHG Emissions.** Beginning on January 2, 2011, new and modified major stationary sources that emit more than 75,000 tons per year of CO_2-equivalent greenhouse gases were required to obtain Prevention of Significant Deterioration (PSD) permits addressing their GHG emissions. These permits, which are mandated under Section 165 of the Clean Air Act, require the applicants to install the Best Available Control Technology (BACT) in order to construct or operate *new and modified* major sources of emissions. State permitting authorities determine what technologies qualify as BACT on a case-by-case basis, using generic guidance issued by EPA on November 10, 2010.[32] The PSD/BACT requirement initially applied only to facilities such as power plants large enough to already be required to obtain PSD permits as a result of their emissions of other pollutants such as sulfur dioxide or nitrogen oxides. What was new starting January 2, 2011, was the addition of GHGs to the list of pollutants that must be addressed by BACT. On July 1, 2011, Step 2 of the requirements took effect: under Step 2, all new and modified sources emitting more than the threshold amounts of GHGs will be required to obtain permits, whether or not they would be required to do so because of emissions of other pollutants.

Existing sources that are already required to obtain operating permits under Title V of the act will also have to provide information on their GHG emissions. EPA notes that the Title V requirement will generally be satisfied by referencing information already provided to EPA under the GHG reporting rule (item 1, above). Title V permits do not impose emission control requirements themselves; they simply summarize emission control requirements mandated by other sections of the Clean Air Act. Thus, the only change to Title V permits will be the addition of GHGs to the list of pollutants that the facilities are allowed to emit. For additional information on PSD and Title V permits, contact Jim McCarthy (7-7225, jmccarthy@crs.loc.gov).

6. **Medium- and Heavy-Duty Vehicle Greenhouse Gas Rule.** On August 9, 2011, EPA and the National Highway Traffic Safety Administration (NHTSA) finalized integrated GHG emission standards and fuel economy standards for medium- and heavy-duty vehicles.[33] EPA's endangerment finding (item 2, above) specifically referenced medium- and heavy-duty trucks as among the sources that contribute to the GHG emissions for which it found endangerment. In addition, NHTSA was required by Section 102 of the Energy Independence and Security Act of 2007 (EISA, P.L. 110-140) to promulgate fuel economy standards for medium- and heavy-duty trucks, reflecting the "maximum feasible improvement" in fuel efficiency. The standards will be phased in between 2014 and 2018. When fully implemented, they will require an average per vehicle reduction in GHG emissions of 17% for diesel trucks and 12% for gasoline-powered trucks. The expected cost increase for the 2014-2018 vehicles affected by the rule is $8.1 billion.

(...continued)

2012.

[32] U.S. Environmental Protection Agency, Office of Air Quality Planning and Standards, "PSD and Title V Permitting Guidance for Greenhouse Gases," November 2010 (subsequently revised, March 2011), at http://www.epa.gov/nsr/ghgdocs/ghgpermittingguidance.pdf.

[33] U.S. Environmental Protection Agency, U.S. Department of Transportation, "Greenhouse Gas Emissions Standards and Fuel Efficiency Standards for Medium- and Heavy-Duty Engines and Vehicles; Final Rules," 76 *Federal Register* 57106, September 15, 2011.

EPA projects benefits of $57 billion over the trucks' lifetimes, including $50 billion in fuel savings. For additional information, contact Brent Yacobucci (7-9662, byacobucci@crs.loc.gov).

7. NSPS for Petroleum Refineries. On December 23, 2010, EPA announced that it was settling a lawsuit filed by 11 states, two municipalities, and three environmental groups over its 2008 decision not to establish New Source Performance Standards (NSPS) for GHG emissions from petroleum refineries. According to the agency, refineries are the second-largest direct stationary source of GHGs in the United States and there are cost-effective strategies for reducing these emissions. The agency agreed to propose NSPS for new refinery facilities and emissions guidelines for existing facilities by December 10, 2011, and to make a final decision on the proposed actions by November 10, 2012. As of April 2012, the standards had not been proposed. For additional information, contact Brent Yacobucci (7-9662, byacobucci@crs.loc.gov) or Jim McCarthy (7-7225, jmccarthy@crs.loc.gov).

Two other rules affecting GHG emissions are under consideration at EPA: NSPS for GHG emissions from electric generating units (item 15, below) and similar standards for Portland cement manufacturing facilities (discussed in item 19, below)

Renewable Fuels

8. Expanded Renewable Fuel Standard (RFS2). On March 26, 2010, EPA promulgated new rules for the renewable fuel standard (RFS) that was expanded by the Energy Independence and Security Act of 2007 (EISA, P.L. 110-140).[34] In 2010, the RFS required the use of 12.95 billion gallons of ethanol and other biofuels in transportation fuel. Within that mandate, the statute required the use of 0.95 billion gallons of advanced biofuels (fuels other than corn starch ethanol), including 100 million gallons of cellulosic biofuels. EISA also requires that advanced biofuels (as well as conventional biofuels from newly built refineries) meet certain lifecycle greenhouse gas reduction requirements. Because no commercial-scale cellulosic biofuel refineries have begun operation, the March 2010 rules reduced the mandated 2010 level for these fuels from 100 million gallons to 6.5 million gallons. The final rule also modified EPA's proposed methodology for measuring lifecycle greenhouse gas emissions. On December 21, 2010, EPA finalized the mandate for 2011.[35] Because of a similar shortfall in projected cellulosic production capacity for 2011, the mandate was waived from 250 million gallons to 6.6 million gallons. The overall mandate of 13.95 billion gallons for 2011 was maintained. For 2012, the 500 million gallon cellulosic mandate was waived to 8.65 million, while the overall mandate of 15.2 billion gallons is maintained.[36] For additional information, contact Brent Yacobucci (7-9662, byacobucci@crs.loc.gov).

9. Ethanol Blend Wall Waiver. On March 6, 2009, Growth Energy (on behalf of 52 U.S. ethanol producers) applied to EPA for a waiver from the current Clean Air Act limitation on ethanol content in gasoline. Ethanol content in gasoline has been capped at 10% (E10); the application requested an increase in the maximum concentration to 15% (E15). A waiver would allow the use

---

[34] U.S. Environmental Protection Agency, "Regulation of Fuels and Fuel Additives: Changes to Renewable Fuel Standard Program; Final Rule," 75 Federal Register 14670-14904, March 26, 2010.

[35] U.S. Environmental Protection Agency, "Regulation of Fuels and Fuel Additives: Modifications to Renewable Fuel Standard Program; Final Rule," 75 *Federal Register* 79964, December 21, 2010.

[36] U.S. Environmental Protection Agency, "Regulation of Fuels and Fuel Additives: 2012 Renewable Fuel Standards: Final Rule," 77 *Federal Register* 1320-1358, January 9, 2012.

of significantly more ethanol in gasoline than has been permitted under the Clean Air Act. Limiting ethanol content to 10% leads to an upper bound of roughly 15 billion gallons of ethanol in all U.S. gasoline. This "blend wall" could limit the fuel industry's ability to meet the Energy Independence and Security Act's future requirements to use increasing amounts of renewable fuels (including ethanol) in transportation.

On November 4, 2010, EPA granted a partial waiver allowing the use of E15 in Model Year (MY) 2007 vehicles and newer.[37] The agency delayed a decision on MY2001-2006 vehicles until the Department of Energy completed testing of those vehicles. On January 21, 2011, EPA announced that the waiver would be expanded to include MY2001-2006 vehicles.[38] EPA determined that data were insufficient to address concerns that had been raised over emissions from MY2000 and older vehicles, as well as heavy-duty vehicles, motorcycles and nonroad applications, and thus a waiver for these vehicles/engines was denied. EPA has noted that granting the waiver eliminates only one impediment to the use of E15—other factors, including retail and blending infrastructure, state and local laws and regulations, and manufacturers' warranties, would still need to be addressed. Because of concerns over potential damage by E15 to equipment not designed for its use, this partial waiver has been challenged in court by a group of vehicle and engine manufacturers. On June 23, 2011, EPA issued final rules, including new labeling requirements, to prevent the accidental use of E15 in vehicles and engines not approved for its use. For additional information, contact Brent Yacobucci (7-9662, byacobucci@crs.loc.gov).

Ambient Air Quality Standards

10. **Ozone Ambient Air Quality Standards.** On January 19, 2010, EPA proposed a revision of the National Ambient Air Quality Standard (NAAQS) for ozone.[39] At the President's request, on September 2, 2011, this proposal was withdrawn, leaving EPA to enforce previously implemented ozone standards.

NAAQS are the cornerstone of the Clean Air Act, in effect defining what EPA considers to be clean air. They do not directly limit emissions, but they set in motion a process under which "nonattainment areas" are identified and states and EPA develop plans and regulations to reduce pollution in those areas. Nonattainment designations may also trigger statutory requirements, including that new major sources offset certain emissions by reducing emissions from existing sources. Currently, there are NAAQS for six pollutants (ozone, particulate matter, sulfur dioxide, carbon monoxide, nitrogen dioxide, and lead). The Clean Air Act requires that these standards be reviewed every five years, and all of the standards have been under court-ordered deadlines for review. EPA last completed a review of the ozone NAAQS in 2008, and made the standard more stringent; but the Obama Administration's EPA suspended implementation of the 2008 standard in 2009 in order to consider further strengthening it.

---

[37] U.S. Environmental Protection Agency, "Partial Grant and Partial Denial of Clean Air Act Waiver Application Submitted by Growth Energy to Increase the Allowable Ethanol Content of Gasoline to 15 Percent; Decision of the Administrator; Notice," 75 *Federal Register* 68094-68150, November 4, 2010.

[38] U.S. Environmental Protection Agency, "Partial Grant of Clean Air Act Waiver Application Submitted by Growth Energy to Increase the Allowable Ethanol Content of Gasoline to 15 Percent; Decision of the Administrator," 76 *Federal Register* 4662, January 26, 2011.

[39] U.S. Environmental Protection Agency, "National Ambient Air Quality Standards for Ozone; Proposed Rule," 75 *Federal Register* 2938, January 19, 2010.

The reconsidered ozone NAAQS that was proposed in January 2010 has been among the most controversial standards under consideration at EPA, because of its wide reach and potential cost. In the 2010 proposal, EPA identified at least 515 counties that would violate the NAAQS if the most recent three years of data available at the time of proposal were used to determine attainment (compared to 85 counties that violated the standard in effect at that time). The agency estimated that the costs of implementing the reconsidered ozone NAAQS, as proposed, would range from $19 billion to $90 billion annually in 2020, with benefits of roughly the same amount.

EPA completed its reconsideration of the ozone NAAQS and sent a final decision to the Office of Management and Budget for interagency review in July 2011. On September 2, 2011, the White House announced that the President had requested that EPA Administrator Jackson withdraw the draft ozone standards at this time. The President's statement noted that work is already underway to update a 2006 review of the science that will result in the reconsideration of the ozone standard in 2013, and stated that he did not support asking state and local governments to begin implementing a new standard that will soon be reconsidered.[40] For additional information, contact Jim McCarthy (7-7225, jmccarthy@crs.loc.gov).

11. Particulate Matter (including "Farm Dust") NAAQS. EPA last completed a review of the NAAQS for particulate matter in 2006. Thus, the agency was required by the Clean Air Act to conduct a review of the standards in 2011. EPA considers particulate matter to be among the most serious air pollutants, responsible for tens of thousands of premature deaths annually.

The current NAAQS sets standards for both "fine" particulates ($PM_{2.5}$) and larger, "coarse" particles (PM_{10}). The $PM_{2.5}$ standards affect far more people and far more counties than the standard for PM_{10}, and both sets of standards have affected mostly industrial, urban areas. Nevertheless, agricultural interests have made substantial efforts over the last year to assail a supposed EPA plan to regulate emissions of farm dust through the PM_{10} NAAQS review, and have urged Congress to prevent the agency from doing so. The House passed legislation, H.R. 1633, to prevent EPA from regulating most sources of rural dust, in December 2011. Thus far, the agency has not proposed any changes to the existing standards, and it has revised its target date for proposal several times, most recently to June 2012. Final standards are not likely to be promulgated before 2013. For additional information, contact Rob Esworthy (7-7236, resworthy@crs.loc.gov).

12. Sulfur Dioxide NAAQS. Three other NAAQS reviews (for sulfur dioxide,[41] nitrogen dioxide,[42] and carbon monoxide) were completed in 2010 and 2011. Of these, only the sulfur dioxide (SO_2) NAAQS is considered an economically significant rule.[43] EPA estimated the cost of the more stringent SO_2 NAAQS at $1.8 billion to $6.8 billion annually, with benefits 5-6 times that amount. For additional information, contact Jim McCarthy (7-7225, jmccarthy@crs.loc.gov).

---

[40] The White House, Office of the Press Secretary, "Statement by the President on the Ozone National Ambient Air Quality Standards," September 2, 2011.

[41] U.S. Environmental Protection Agency, "Primary National Ambient Air Quality Standard for Sulfur Dioxide; Final Rule," 75 *Federal Register* 35520, June 22, 2010.

[42] U.S. Environmental Protection Agency, "Primary National Ambient Air Quality Standards for Nitrogen Dioxide; Final Rule," 75 *Federal Register* 6473, February 9, 2010.

[43] The agency concluded that the nitrogen dioxide NAAQS, even though it was strengthened, would have no costs or benefits, since the agency projected no areas to be nonattainment for the revised standard. The agency decided not to change the carbon monoxide NAAQS, so there were no costs or benefits associated with that review, either.

Electric Generating Units

13. **Cross-State Air Pollution (Clean Air Transport) Rule.** EPA's major clean air initiative under the Bush Administration, the Clean Air Interstate Rule (CAIR), was vacated and remanded to the agency by the D.C. Circuit Court of Appeals in 2008. EPA promulgated a replacement for the rule, which it calls the Cross-State Air Pollution Rule, August 8, 2011.[44] The original rule, designed to control emissions of air pollution that causes air quality problems in downwind states, established cap-and-trade programs for sulfur dioxide and nitrogen oxide emissions from coal-fired electric power plants in 28 eastern states, at an estimated annual cost of $3.6 billion in 2015. The replacement rule also applies to 28 states; it allows unlimited intrastate allowance trading, but limits interstate trading in response to the D.C. Circuit decision; its annual compliance cost is estimated at $3.0 billion in 2012 and $2.4 billion in 2014. EPA estimates the benefits of the rule at $120 billion to $280 billion annually, chiefly the avoidance of 13,000 to 34,000 annual premature deaths. Because of the earlier CAIR requirements, electric generators have already achieved more than two-thirds of the pollution reductions necessary to comply with the 2014 standards. For additional information, contact Jim McCarthy (7-7225, jmccarthy@crs.loc.gov).

14. **Mercury and Air Toxics Standards / MACT for Electric Generating Units ("Utility MACT").** In 2005, EPA promulgated regulations establishing a cap-and-trade system to limit emissions of mercury from coal-fired power plants. The rules were challenged, and the D.C. Circuit Court of Appeals vacated them in 2008. Rather than appeal the ruling to the Supreme Court, EPA agreed to propose and promulgate Maximum Achievable Control Technology (MACT) standards by the end of 2011. The standards for existing units, promulgated February 16, 2012,[45] can be met by 56% of coal- and oil-fired electric generating units using pollution control equipment already installed; the other 44% would be required to install technology that will reduce uncontrolled mercury and acid gas emissions by about 90%, at an annual cost of $9.6 billion. Standards for new facilities are more stringent, and many (including the industry that manufactures pollution control and monitoring equipment), doubt whether compliance with the mercury portion of these standards can be measured. EPA estimates that the annual benefits, including the avoidance of up to 11,000 premature deaths annually, will be between $37 billion and $90 billion. Following promulgation of these standards, existing power plants will have three years, with a possible one-year extension, to meet the standards. About 20 states have already established mercury emission control standards for coal-fired power plants, and other major sources have been controlled for as long as 15 years, reducing their emissions as much as 95%. For additional information, contact Jim McCarthy (7-7225, jmccarthy@crs.loc.gov).

15. **NSPS for GHG Emissions from Electric Generating Units.** EPA has stated for some time that it would undertake a review of the New Source Performance Standards (NSPS) to consider greenhouse gas emission standards for electric generating units at the same time as it developed the electric utility MACT standards. Electric generating units are the largest U.S. source of both greenhouse gas and mercury emissions, accounting for about one-third of all GHG emissions in

---

[44] U.S. Environmental Protection Agency, "Federal Implementation Plans: Interstate Transport of Fine Particulate Matter and Ozone and Correction of SIP Approvals," 76 *Federal Register* 48208, August 8, 2011. Explanatory material can be found at http://www.epa.gov/crossstaterule/actions.html. The rule was generally referred to as the Clean Air Transport Rule prior to being finalized.

[45] U.S. Environmental Protection Agency, "National Emission Standards for Hazardous Air Pollutants from Coal and Oil-Fired Electric Utility Steam Generating Units and Standards of Performance for Fossil-Fuel-Fired Electric Utility, Industrial-Commercial-Institutional, and Small Industrial-Commercial-Institutional Steam Generating Units," 77 *Federal Register* 9304, February 16, 2012.

addition to about half of U.S. mercury emissions. In a settlement agreement with 11 states and other parties, EPA agreed to propose the NSPS for power plants by July 26, 2011, and take final action on the proposal by May 26, 2012. This schedule has encountered delays: proposed standards were not released until March 27, 2012,[46] and the final standards are likely to be delayed as well.

EPA set the proposed GHG emission standards at a level achievable by uncontrolled natural-gas-fired units or by coal-fired units using carbon capture and storage (CCS) technology. Although the components of CCS technology have been demonstrated, no existing power plant combines them all in an operating unit, and the electric power industry has generally concluded that a CCS requirement would effectively prohibit the construction of new coal-fired plants, other than those already permitted. EPA maintains otherwise, but it also says that, because of low natural gas prices and abundant existing generation capacity, it believes no new coal-fired units subject to the proposed standards will be constructed between now and 2020. For additional information, contact Jim McCarthy (7-7225, jmccarthy@crs.loc.gov).

Boilers and Incinerators

16.-17. MACT and Area Source Standards for Boilers. EPA proposed Maximum Achievable Control Technology standards to control emissions of toxic air pollutants from commercial and industrial boilers in June 2010. A final rule was issued February 21, 2011, under a court order by the Federal District Court for the District of Columbia.[47] Because of voluminous comments and new information received from industry during a public comment period, EPA had asked the court to extend the deadline for promulgating final standards to April 2012. Having been denied that extension, the agency issued a statement saying, "The standards will be significantly different than what EPA proposed.... The agency believes these changes still deserve further public review and comment and expects to solicit further comment through a reconsideration of the rules."[48] The agency initiated a reconsideration after it released the final rule, and it proposed changes to the rule December 2, 2011, stating that it expected promulgation of changes by April 30, 2012. However, as of this writing, the rules had not gone to OMB for final review.

Boilers are used throughout industry and in many commercial and institutional facilities. The D.C. Circuit vacated EPA's previous MACT rule for this category in 2007, saying EPA had wrongly excluded many industrial boilers from the definition of solid waste incinerators, which have more stringent emissions requirements under the Clean Air Act. The vacated rule had estimated annual costs of $837 million, with a benefit-cost ratio of about 20 to 1. The February 2011 rule would set more stringent standards. It would affect 13,840 boilers, according to the agency, with annual costs estimated at $1.4 billion and benefits of $22 billion to $54 billion annually, including the avoidance of 2,500 to 6,500 premature deaths.

---

[46] As of mid-April, the standards had not appeared in the *Federal Register*, but a pre-publication copy and supporting materials are available at http://www.epa.gov/carbonpollutionstandard/actions.html.

[47] The final rule appeared in the *Federal Register* March 21, 2011. U.S. Environmental Protection Agency, "National Emission Standards for Hazardous Air Pollutants for Major Sources: Industrial, Commercial, and Institutional Boilers and Process Heaters; Final Rule," 76 *Federal Register* 15608, March 21, 2011.

[48] U.S. EPA, "EPA Announces Next Steps on Emissions Standards for Boilers, Certain Incinerators," Press Release, January 20, 2011, at http://yosemite.epa.gov/opa/admpress.nsf/6424ac1caa800aab85257359003f5337/58f5bee5e13c61228525781e007e9881.

EPA also promulgated what are called "area source" standards for smaller boilers at the same time as the MACT.[49] The area source standards would affect 187,000 boilers, most of which would only be required to perform a tune-up every two years to comply with the regulations. EPA estimated the net cost of the area source rule to be $487 million annually, with partial benefits ranging from $210 million to $520 million annually. For additional information, contact Jim McCarthy (7-7225, jmccarthy@crs.loc.gov).

18. **Commercial and Industrial Solid Waste Incinerator (CISWI) Standards.** A third regulation promulgated at the same time as the boiler MACT and area source boiler rules would set standards for emissions from commercial and industrial solid waste incinerators.[50] These standards are related to the D.C. Circuit's remand of the boiler rules in 2007, and also faced a judicial deadline of February 21, 2011. The rules would expand the number of existing facilities subject to the more stringent CISWI standards from 20 to 88, with annual costs of $232 million, according to EPA, and benefits of $360 million-$870 million annually. EPA is also reconsidering these rules, on the same schedule as the Boiler MACT, and released proposed revisions to the standards December 2, 2011. For additional information, contact Jim McCarthy (7-7225, jmccarthy@crs.loc.gov).

Other

19. **Emission Standards for Portland Cement Manufacturing.** On September 9, 2010, EPA promulgated New Source Performance Standards (NSPS) for conventional pollutants from new cement kilns and Maximum Achievable Control Technology standards for hazardous air pollutants from both existing and new cement kilns.[51] When fully implemented in 2013, the standards will require a 92% reduction in emissions of both particulate matter and mercury and a 97% reduction in emissions of acid gases, according to EPA, as well as controlling other pollutants. EPA had previously issued emission standards for this industry in 1999, but the standards were challenged in court and remanded to the agency by the D.C. Circuit Court of Appeals. The new rules reflect EPA's reconsideration of the standards.

The agency estimates that it will cost the industry $350 million annually to comply with the standards, but that benefits (including the avoidance of 960 to 2,500 premature deaths in people with heart disease) will be worth $6.7 billion to $18 billion annually. The trade association representing the industry says the standards will cause some facilities to close. On December 9, 2011, the D.C. Circuit Court of Appeals remanded the 2010 standards to EPA for the agency to reconsider emission standards for kilns that use solid waste as fuel. The court did not stay implementation of the 2010 standards, however.

Further regulation of this industry, which is the third highest U.S. source of carbon dioxide emissions, is under consideration: when EPA promulgated the rule in September 2010, it stated in

---

[49] U.S. Environmental Protection Agency, "National Emission Standards for Hazardous Air Pollutants for Area Sources: Industrial, Commercial, and Institutional Boilers; Final Rule," 76 *Federal Register* 15554, March 21, 2011.

[50] U.S. Environmental Protection Agency, "Standards of Performance for New Stationary Sources and Emission Guidelines for Existing Sources: Commercial and Industrial Solid Waste Incineration Units; Final Rule," 76 *Federal Register* 15704, March 21, 2011.

[51] U.S. Environmental Protection Agency, "National Emission Standards for Hazardous Air Pollutants from the Portland Cement Manufacturing Industry and Standards of Performance for Portland Cement Plants; Final Rule," 75 *Federal Register* 54970, September 9, 2010.

the rule's preamble to the rule that it is "working towards a proposal for GHG standards" for these plants.[52] For additional information, contact Jim McCarthy (7-7225, jmccarthy@crs.loc.gov).

20.-21. Stationary Internal Combustion Engines. EPA set standards for both compression-ignition[53] (generally diesel) and spark ignition (generally gasoline) stationary engines[54] in 2010. The regulations would affect stationary engines, such as emergency power generators used by hospitals and other sources and electric power generators used for compressors and pumps by a wide array of industrial, agricultural, and oil and gas industry sources. The rules are referred to as the RICE (Reciprocating Internal Combustion Engine) rules. They apply to engines that meet specific siting, age, and size criteria (generally engines of 500 horsepower or less). EPA estimates that more than 1.2 million engines will be affected by the regulations. Depending on the type of engine, owners will have to install pollution control equipment or follow certain work practice standards, such as burning low sulfur fuel or performing oil changes and inspections. EPA estimates the health benefits of the two rules will be between $1.45 billion and $3.5 billion annually by 2013. Annualized costs for the rules are estimated to be $626 million in 2013. In response to a suit by the Engine Manufacturers Association, on November 2, 2011, EPA agreed to revise a portion of the spark ignition rule dealing with formaldehyde emissions. For additional information, contact Jim McCarthy (7-7225, jmccarthy@crs.loc.gov).

22.-23. Ocean-Going Ships. EPA took two steps to control emissions from ocean-going ships in 2009 and 2010. It promulgated emission standards for new marine engines[55] and it proposed the establishment of Emission Control Areas extending 200 nautical miles off most U.S. shores.[56] In the Emission Control Areas (ECAs), which received final approval in March 2010, both U.S. and foreign ships would be required to use low sulfur fuel. In both cases, the actions reflect international standards that the United States and other maritime nations have agreed to under the International Convention for the Prevention of Pollution from Ships (MARPOL). EPA estimated the cost of these two initiatives at over $3 billion annually by 2030, mostly attributable to the cleaner fuel requirement. The agency also estimated that monetized benefits of the requirements will exceed costs by more than 30 to 1. The Emission Control Areas and the new standards were supported by both industry and environmental groups. For additional information, contact Jim McCarthy (7-7225, jmccarthy@crs.loc.gov).

24. Oil and Natural Gas Air Pollution Standards. In February 2010, EPA signed a consent agreement under which it was to promulgate revisions of the New Source Performance Standards and Hazardous Air Pollutant standards for oil and gas production by November 30, 2011. The agency finalized these rules on April 17, 2012.[57] Under the CAA, EPA is required to review New Source Performance Standards every eight years; the revisions update NSPS rules for VOCs and

---

[52] Ibid., p. 54997.

[53] U.S. Environmental Protection Agency, "National Emission Standards for Hazardous Air Pollutants: Reciprocating Internal Combustion Engines; Final Rule," 75 *Federal Register* 9648, March 3, 2010.

[54] U.S. Environmental Protection Agency, "National Emission Standards for Hazardous Air Pollutants for Reciprocating Internal Combustion Engines; Final Rule," 75 *Federal Register* 51570, August 20, 2010.

[55] U.S. Environmental Protection Agency, "Control of Emissions from New Marine Compression-Ignition Engines at or Above 30 Liters per Cylinder; Final Rule," 75 *Federal Register* 22896, April 30, 2010.

[56] International Maritime Organization, Marine Environmental Protection Committee, "Proposal to Designate an Emission Control Area for Nitrogen Oxides, Sulphur Oxides and Particulate Matter, Submitted by the United States and Canada," April 2, 2009, at http://www.epa.gov/oms/regs/nonroad/marine/ci/mepc-59-eca-proposal.pdf.

[57] For information, see http://www.epa.gov/airquality/oilandgas/actions.html.

SO2 that were promulgated in 1985. Similarly, EPA had a statutory obligation to review hazardous air pollutant standards for oil and natural production, which were issued in 1999, by 2007. Additionally, the 2012 rules are the first regulations to address emissions from natural gas wells that use hydraulic fracturing ("fracking"). The new standards, which will be fully implemented by 2015, will require companies to capture natural gas and volatile organic compounds (VOCs) that escape when hydraulically fractured gas wells are prepared for production. The rules affect production, processing, transmission, and storage, but not distribution to customers. EPA estimates that the rules will result in the capture of 95% of the VOCs and methane otherwise emitted. Although there are costs associated with the use of equipment to capture the emissions, EPA estimates that the rules will produce a net annual savings of $11 million to $19 million for the industry, because the captured gas and condensate can be sold. Some states already require similar measures, and EPA estimates that about half of fracked natural gas wells already meet the standards. For additional information, contact Rick Lattanzio (7-1754, rlattanzio@crs.loc.gov).

25. **Tier 3 Emissions Standards for Passenger Cars and Light Trucks and Gasoline Standards.** In February 2011, EPA began to scope out new emissions standards for conventional pollutants (i.e., non-greenhouse gases) from passenger cars and light trucks. In a May 2010 memorandum from the White House to the EPA and NHTSA Administrators, President Obama directed EPA to review the adequacy of the current "Tier 2" emissions standards for these vehicles, which EPA finalized in February 2000, and were phased in between MY2004 and MY2009.[58] As with the Tier 2 standards, the proposed Tier 3 standards are expected to include changes to both vehicle emissions standards, as well as changes to rules on fuel formulation that will allow the use of new technology. (To permit the use of more advanced emissions controls for Tier 2, EPA also finalized tighter gasoline sulfur standards.) EPA projects that the agency will publish a proposed rule in July 2012. In a letter to EPA Administrator Jackson, several Senators asked EPA to delay its rulemaking over concerns that the new fuel standards would raise the price of gasoline.[59] For additional information, contact Brent Yacobucci (7-9662, byacobucci@crs.loc.gov).

Clean Water Act

26. **Construction Site Effluent Limitation Guidelines.** On December 1, 2009, EPA promulgated regulations under the Clean Water Act (CWA), called effluent limitation guidelines (ELGs), to limit pollution from stormwater runoff at construction sites.[60] The rule, called the Construction and Development ELG, took effect February 1, 2010. OMB determined that it is an economically significant rule. It requires construction sites that disturb one or more acres of land to use erosion and sediment control best management practices to ensure that soil disturbed during construction activity does not pollute nearby waterbodies. For construction sites disturbing 10 acres or more, the rule established, for the first time, enforceable numeric limits on stormwater runoff pollution. EPA issued the rule in response to a 2004 lawsuit filed by an environmental group; in 2006, a federal court ordered EPA to issue a final rule by December 1, 2009. The rule affects about

---

[58] For more information on the Tier 2 standards, see CRS Report RS20247, *EPA's Tier 2 Emission Standards for New Motor Vehicles A Fact Sheet*, by David M. Bearden.

[59] Jeremy P. Jacobs, "Bipartisan Senate Group Seeks Delay in EPA Tailpipe Rules," *E&E News PM*, January 12, 2012.

[60] U.S. Environmental Protection Agency, "Effluent Limitation Guidelines for the Construction and Development Point Source Category," 74 *Federal Register* 62996-63058, December 1, 2009.

82,000 firms nationwide involved in residential, commercial, highway, street, and bridge construction. EPA has issued effluent guidelines for 56 industries that include many types of discharges, such as manufacturing and service industries. These guidelines are implemented in discharge permits issued by states and EPA. Several industry groups challenged the Construction and Development ELG. In response, EPA examined the data set underlying a portion of the rule and concluded that it improperly interpreted the data. In August 2010, a federal appeals court granted EPA's request for remand of a portion of the rule to conduct a rulemaking to correct the numeric effluent limitation. In November 2010, EPA promulgated a direct final rule to stay the effectiveness of the numeric turbidity limit in the 2009 rule; other portions of the rule remain in effect.[61] In January 2012, EPA published a Federal Register Notice seeking data on the effectiveness of technologies in controlling turbidity in discharges from construction sites, information that the agency intends to use in revising the rule, which it expects to finalize by November 19, 2012.[62] For additional information, contact Claudia Copeland (7-7227, ccopeland@crs.loc.gov).

27. **Pesticide Application General Permit.** EPA has developed a CWA general permit to control pesticides that are applied to waters of the United States, such as aerial application of insecticide to control mosquitoes. The general permit was issued on October 31, 2011, in response to a 2009 federal court decision that invalidated a 2006 EPA rule, which had codified the agency's long-standing view that pesticide applications that comply with federal pesticides law do not require CWA permits.[63] The estimated universe of affected activities is approximately 5.6 million applications annually, which are performed by 365,000 applicators, in four use patterns: mosquito and other flying insect pest control, aquatic weed and algae control, aquatic nuisance animal control, and forest canopy pest control. The permit requires all operators covered by the permit to minimize pesticide discharges to waters by practices such as using the lowest amount of pesticide product that is optimal for controlling the target pest. It also requires operators to prepare plans to document their pest management practices. Under OMB's criteria, the permit is not a significant rule, but is "economically significant."[64] Meanwhile, in March 2011, the House passed legislation (H.R. 872) intended to overturn the court's 2009 ruling by exempting aerial pesticide application activities from clean water permit requirements. The Senate Agriculture Committee also has approved H.R. 872.[65] For additional information, contact Claudia Copeland (7-7227, ccopeland@crs.loc.gov).

28. **Florida Nutrient Water Quality Standards.** The CWA directs states to adopt water quality standards for their waters and authorizes EPA to promulgate new or revised standards if a state's

---

[61] U.S. Environmental Protection Agency, "Direct Final Rule Staying Numeric Limitation for the Construction and Development Point Source Category," 75 *Federal Register* 68215-68217, November 5, 2010.

[62] U.S. Environmental Protection Agency, "Effluent Limitations Guidelines and Standards for the Construction and Development Point Source Category; Notice," 77 *Federal Register* 112, January 3, 2012.

[63] U.S. Environmental Protection Agency, "Final National Pollutant Discharge Elimination System (NPDES) General Permit for Point Source Discharges from the Application of Pesticides; Notice of final permit," 76 *Federal Register* 68750-68756, November 7, 2011.

[64] "Significant" rules are a broader OMB category that includes not only the economically significant (i.e., primarily those with an annual effect on the economy of $100 million or more), but also rules that "create a serious inconsistency or otherwise interfere with an action taken or planned by another agency"; "materially alter the budgetary impact of entitlements, grants, user fees, or loan programs or the rights and obligations of recipients thereof"; or "raise novel legal or policy issues arising out of legal mandates, the President's priorities, or the principles set forth" in Executive Order 12866.

[65] For additional information, see CRS Report RL32884, *Pesticide Use and Water Quality Are the Laws Complementary or in Conflict?*, by Claudia Copeland.

actions fail to meet CWA requirements. Water quality standards consist of designated uses, criteria to protect the designated uses, and an antidegradation statement. They serve as the framework for pollution control measures specified for individual sources. Because of severe water quality impairment of Florida waters by nutrients (nitrogen and phosphorus) from diverse sources including agriculture and livestock, municipal and industrial wastewater discharges, and urban stormwater runoff, EPA determined in 2009 that Florida's existing *narrative* water quality standards for nutrients must be revised in the form of *numeric* criteria that will enable Florida to better control nutrient pollution. In 2009 EPA entered into a consent decree with environmental litigants requiring the agency to promulgate numeric nutrient water quality standards for Florida. To meet the legal deadline, EPA promulgated the first phase of these standards, called the "inland waters rule," on December 5, 2010.[66] In response to criticism of the standards, EPA delayed the effective date of the final rule, to allow local governments, businesses, and the state of Florida time to review the standards and develop implementation strategies. EPA further delayed the effective date of the 2010 rule until July 6, 2012, to allow the state to adopt its own numeric nutrient criteria for inland waters, which the state proposed in November 2011.[67] If the state adopts an approvable rule that meets CWA criteria, EPA intends to initiate administrative action to withdraw the 2010 federal rule. Nevertheless, separate legal challenges to the rule have been filed in federal court by environmental advocates, the state of Florida, and others. In February, a federal court ruling largely upheld EPA's authority and methodology in setting numeric criteria for nutrient pollution in Florida waters, but remanded a portion of the rule concerning numeric criteria for streams, saying they were arbitrary and capricious.

Water quality standards do not have the force of law until the state translates them into permit limits or otherwise imposes pollution control requirements on dischargers in the state. The rule will not establish any requirements directly applicable to regulated entities or other sources of nutrient pollution. While few dispute the need to reduce nutrients in Florida's waters, EPA's rule has been controversial, involving disputes about the data underlying the proposal, potential costs of complying with numeric standards when they are incorporated into discharge permit limitations, and disputes over administrative flexibility. EPA estimated that the potential incremental costs associated with the rule range from $16 million to $25 million per year, and monetized benefits of $28 million per year. Many stakeholders contend that EPA greatly underestimated costs. The rule was determined by OMB to be a significant regulatory action, but not "economically significant." In response to criticisms, EPA requested the National Academy of Sciences to review the agency's economic analysis of the costs of state implementation of the rule. The committee's report, released in March, found that EPA underestimated implementation costs and did not adequately consider uncertainties that would affect the cost of changing from narrative to numeric water quality standards.[68]

The second phase of standards, for estuaries, coastal waters and flowing waters in the South Florida Region, currently is due to be proposed by May 21, 2012, and finalized by January 13, 2013. It is conceivable that these dates could change, based on the state of Florida's efforts to

---

[66] U.S. Environmental Protection Agency, "Water Quality Standards for the State of Florida's Lakes and Flowing Waters; Final Rule," 75 *Federal Register* 75762-75807, December 5, 2010.

[67] U.S. Environmental protection Agency, "Effective Date for the Water Quality Standards for the State of Florida's Lakes and Flowing Waters," 76 *Federal Register* 79604, December 22, 2011.

[68] Water Science and Technology Board, Division on Earth and Life Sciences, National Research Council of the National Academies, *Review of the EPA's Economic Analysis of Final Water Quality Standards for Nutrients for Lakes and Flowing Waters in Florida*, March 2012, http://www.nap.edu/catalog.php?record_id=13376.

---

adopt numeric nutrient water quality standards. For additional information, contact Claudia Copeland (7-7227, ccopeland@crs.loc.gov).

29. **Chesapeake Bay TMDL.** Pursuant to a court-ordered schedule, EPA has developed a plan, called a Total Maximum Daily Limit (TMDL), to restore nutrient-impaired waters of the Chesapeake Bay. The TMDL is required because states in the Chesapeake Bay watershed have failed to meet deadlines to attain water quality goals for the Bay, thus triggering Clean Water Act requirements that the federal government must develop a plan to do so. The TMDL is not a regulation. A TMDL represents the maximum amount of a pollutant that a body of water may receive and still meet its water quality standards. Individual actions needed to meet the overall pollutant limits specified in the TMDL, such as discharge permit limits or other controls, are to be developed by the Chesapeake Bay states in Watershed Implementation Plans. The Chesapeake Bay TMDL is the largest ever developed by EPA or any state, since it will apply to all impaired waters of the 64,000 square miles of the six states in the Bay watershed. On December 29, 2010, EPA issued the TMDL.[69] Pursuant to the schedule of steps in the TMDL, states are now developing specific plans called Watershed Implementation Plans (WIPs), which outline the types of controls and best management practices that will be used to reduce pollution in the Bay. EPA approved the first phase WIPs in December 2010, and is now reviewing the jurisdictions' Phase II WIPs, providing greater detail about pollutant reductions planned through the year 2017. The TMDL has been controversial with agricultural and other groups that are concerned about the likely mandatory nature of many of EPA's and states' upcoming actions. A lawsuit challenging EPA's authority to set pollution limits under the multistate TMDL was filed by the American Farm Bureau Federation in January 2011. For additional information, contact Claudia Copeland (7-7227, ccopeland@crs.loc.gov).

30. **"Post-Construction" Stormwater Rule.** EPA is exploring regulatory options to strengthen the existing regulatory program for managing stormwater, which is a significant source of water quality impairments nationwide. Under the current program, large cities and most industry sources are subject to CWA rules issued in 1990; smaller cities, other industrial sources, and construction sites are covered by rules issued in 1999. EPA is considering options to strengthen stormwater regulations, including establishing post-construction requirements for stormwater discharges from new development and redevelopment, which currently are not regulated. The rule is expected to focus on stormwater discharges from developed or post-construction sites such as subdivisions, roadways, industrial facilities and commercial buildings, or shopping centers. In early 2010, EPA held a series of listening sessions across the country as part of a process seeking public comments on potential considerations for regulatory changes. Under a consent agreement with environmental groups, EPA expects to issue a proposed rule by the end of April and to issue a final rule in November 2012. For additional information, contact Claudia Copeland (7-7227, ccopeland@crs.loc.gov).

31. **Revised Cooling Water Intake Rule.** EPA has proposed a CWA rule to protect fish from entrainment by cooling water intake structures at existing power plants and certain other industrial facilities. The proposed rule will revise EPA regulations issued in 2004 that were challenged in federal court by electric utility companies and others and were remanded to EPA by court order in 2007 and rules issued in 2006 that also apply to new offshore oil and gas facilities

---

[69] Notice of the TMDL appeared in the *Federal Register* January 5, 2011. U.S. Environmental Protection Agency, "Clean Water Act Section 303(d): Notice for the Establishment of the Total Maximum Daily Load (TMDL) for the Chesapeake Bay," 76 *Federal Register* 549-550, January 5, 2011.

and existing manufacturing facilities, which EPA asked a court to remand to the agency for modification.[70] The proposal also responds to a 2009 U.S. Supreme Court ruling which said that, in developing the revised cooling water intake structure rule, EPA can consider the costs and benefits of protecting fish and other aquatic organisms.[71] The rule combines cooling water intake rules that apply to approximately 1,150 existing electric generating and manufacturing plants. On December 3, 2010, a federal court issued an order endorsing terms of a settlement agreement between EPA and environmental groups, establishing deadlines for the agency to propose and finalize a revised cooling water intake rule. EPA proposed the rule on March 28, 2011, and, under the consent decree, is required to take final action by July 27, 2012. Even before release, the proposed rule was highly controversial. Many in industry feared, while environmental groups hoped, that EPA would require installation of technology that most effectively minimizes impacts of cooling water intake structures, but also is the most costly option. The EPA proposal declined to mandate such technology universally and instead favors a less costly, more flexible regulatory option.[72] For additional information, contact Claudia Copeland (7-7227, ccopeland@crs.loc.gov).

32. **Revised Steam Electric Effluent Guidelines**. Under authority of CWA Section 304, EPA establishes national technology-based regulations, called effluent limitation guidelines (ELGs), to reduce pollutant discharges from industries directly to waters of the United States and indirectly to municipal wastewater treatment plants. These requirements are incorporated into discharge permits issued by EPA and states. The current steam electric power plant rules[73] apply to about 1,200 nuclear- and fossil-fueled steam electric power plants nationwide, 500 of which are coal-fired. In a 2009 study, EPA found that these regulations, which were promulgated in 1982, do not adequately address the pollutants being discharged and have not kept pace with changes that have occurred in the electric power industry over the last three decades. Pollutants of concern include metals (e.g., mercury, arsenic, and selenium), nutrients, and total dissolved solids. The rulemaking will address discharges from coal ash storage ponds and flue gas desulfurization (FGD) air pollution controls, as well as other power plant waste streams.[74]

Pursuant to a November 8, 2010, consent decree that it entered into with environmental litigants, EPA agreed to propose the revised power plant ELG by July 23, 2012, and to finalize the rule by January 31, 2014. For additional information, contact Claudia Copeland (7-7227, ccopeland@crs.loc.gov).

33. **Oil Spill Prevention, Control, and Countermeasure Requirements, including deadline extension for farms and exemption for milk storage.** To prevent the discharge of oil from onshore and offshore facilities, EPA issued CWA regulations for spill prevention control and countermeasure (SPCC) plans in 1973.[75] SPCC plans apply to owners or operators of certain non-

---

[70] 40 CFR §125.90 and 40 CFR §125.130.

[71] Entergy Corp. v. Riverkeeper Inc., 129 S. Ct. 1498 (2009).

[72] The rule was published in the Federal Register on April 20. U.S. Environmental Protection Agency, "National Pollutant Discharge Elimination System—Cooling Water Intake Structures at Existing Facilities and Phase 1 Facilities," 76 *Federal Register* 22174-22228, April 20, 2011. For information, see CRS Report R41786, *Cooling Water Intake Structures Summary of EPA's Proposed Rule*, by Claudia Copeland.

[73] 40 CFR §423.10.

[74] Separately, EPA also is considering regulation of coal ash disposal sites under Resource Conservation and Recovery Act, as discussed in this report under "Coal Combustion Waste."

[75] 38 *Federal Register* 34164, December 11, 1973.

transportation-related facilities. In general, SPCC plans focus on oil spill prevention, requiring, for example, secondary containment (e.g., dikes or berms) for oil-storage equipment.

Following the passage of the Oil Pollution Act of 1990, the agency proposed substantial changes and clarifications that were not made final until July 2002.[76] However, EPA has both extended the 2002 rule's compliance date (on multiple occasions) and made further amendments to the 2002 rule. On one occasion, amendments offered by the Bush Administration's EPA in 2008 were eliminated by the Obama Administration's EPA the following year.[77]

For most types of facilities subject to SPCC requirements, the deadline for complying with the changes made in 2002 was November 10, 2011.[78] However, in a November 2011 rulemaking, EPA extended the compliance date for farms to May 10, 2013.[79]

Pursuant to the CWA definition of oil, the SPCC requirements apply to petroleum-based and non-petroleum-based oil.[80] In a 1975 *Federal Register* notice, EPA clarified that its 1973 SPCC regulations apply to oils from animal and vegetable sources.[81] EPA subsequently stated that "milk typically contains a percentage of animal fat, which is a non-petroleum oil" and is thus potentially subject to SPCC provisions.[82] However, in January 2009, EPA proposed a conditional exemption from SPCC requirements for milk storage units.[83] EPA issued a final rule April 18, 2011, exempting all milk and milk product containers and associated piping from the SPCC requirements. EPA's rationale for the exemption is that these units are subject to industry standards for sanitation and may be regulated by other agencies, including the U.S. Department of Agriculture.[84] In addition, the final rule states that exempted milk storage units are not included in a facility's overall oil storage volume, a primary factor for SPCC applicability. For additional information, contact Jonathan Ramseur (7-7919, jramseur@crs.loc.gov).

34. **"Waters of the United States" Interpretive Guidance.** From the earliest days, Congress has grappled with where to set the line between federal and state authority over the nation's waterways. Typically, this debate occurred in the context of federal legislation restricting uses of waterways that impaired navigation and commerce. The phrase Congress often used to specify waterways over which the federal government had authority was "navigable waters of the United States." However, in the legislation that became the CWA of 1972, Congress felt that the term was too constricted to define the reach of a law whose purpose was not maintaining navigability, as in the past, but rather preventing pollution. Accordingly, in the CWA Congress retained the traditional term "navigable waters," but defined it broadly to mean "waters of the United States."

---

[76] 67 *Federal Register* 47041, July 17, 2002.

[77] A November 13, 2009 rule (74 *Federal Register* 58784) eliminated specific exclusions/exemptions made by a December 5, 2008 rulemaking (73 *Federal Register* 74236).

[78] U.S. Environmental Protection Agency, "Oil Pollution Prevention; Spill Prevention, Control, and Countermeasure Rule Compliance Date Amendment ," 75 *Federal Register* 63093, October 14, 2010.

[79] U.S. Environmental Protection Agency, "Oil Pollution Prevention: Spill Prevention, Control, and Countermeasure Rule—Compliance Date Amendment for Farms," 76 *Federal Register* 72120, November 22, 2011.

[80] See CWA Section 311(a) (33 U.S.C. 1321(a)).

[81] 40 *Federal Register* 28849, July 9, 1975.

[82] 74 *Federal Register* 2461, January 15, 2009.

[83] U.S. Environmental Protection Agency, "Oil Pollution Prevention: Spill Prevention, Control, and Countermeasure Rule Requirements—Amendments," 74 *Federal Register* 2461, January 15, 2009.

[84] 76 *Federal Register* 21652, April 18, 2011.

That phrase is important in the context of Section 404 of the law, a permit program jointly administered by EPA and the Army Corps of Engineers that regulates discharges of dredged and fill material to U.S. waters, including wetlands. The same phrase also defines the geographic extent of the other parts of the CWA, including state-established water quality standards, the discharge permit program in Section 402, oil spill liability, and enforcement. Consequently, how broadly or narrowly "waters of the United States" is defined has been a central question of CWA law and policy for nearly 40 years.

Controversies increased following two Supreme Court rulings, one in 2001 and one in 2006, on how "waters of the United States" are defined for purposes of the 404/wetlands permit program. Those two rulings left many uncertainties about their interpretation, uncertainties that first the Bush Administration and now the Obama Administration have attempted to clarify through a series of interpretive guidance documents. Most recently, in April 2011, EPA and the Army Corps jointly proposed new guidance in an effort to clarify the geographic reach of federal regulation, in light of the law, the Court's rulings, and science. Under the new guidance, federal protection of water quality would apply to more waters than currently are considered jurisdictional—a conclusion that has pleased some and alarmed others.[85] The proposed guidance was subject to public comment until July 31, 2011. At some point—either after the guidance is finalized or in lieu of final guidance—the agencies expect to propose revisions to their regulations to further clarify which waters are subject to CWA jurisdiction, consistent with the Supreme Court's rulings, but there is no schedule for when this will occur.[86] For additional information, contact Claudia Copeland (7-7227, ccopeland@crs.loc.gov).

35. **Mountaintop Mining in Appalachia.** EPA and other federal agencies (the Office of Surface Mining and Reclamation, in the Department of the Interior; and the U.S. Army Corps of Engineers) are developing a series of actions and regulatory proposals to reduce the harmful environmental and health impacts of surface coal mining, including mountaintop removal mining, in Appalachia. The actions, announced in a June 2009 interagency Memorandum of Understanding, are intended to improve regulation and strengthen environmental reviews of permit requirements under the CWA and the Surface Mining Control and Reclamation Act (SMCRA). Viewed broadly, the Administration's combined actions on mountaintop mining displease both industry and environmental advocates. The additional scrutiny of permits and more stringent requirements have angered the coal industry and many of its supporters. At the same time, while environmental groups support EPA's steps to restrict the practice, many favor tougher requirements or even total rejection of mountaintop mining in Appalachia. Many of the actions have been highly controversial in Congress.

EPA is a key participant in several of the actions. In 2009 EPA and the Corps began conducting detailed evaluations of 79 pending CWA permit applications for surface mining activities in order to limit environmental impacts of the proposed activities under a process called Enhanced Coordination Procedures (ECP). Coal industry groups and coal state officials contended that the ECP process resulted in costly delay in issuance of permits. They challenged the process in federal court, and in October 2011, the court struck down the ECP as an unlawful transfer of legal

---

[85] Environmental Protection Agency and Army Corps of Engineers, "Draft Guidance on Identifying Waters Protected by the Clean Water Act," April 27, 2011, p. 2, http://water.epa.gov/lawsregs/guidance/wetlands/upload/wous_guidance_4-2011.pdf.

[86] For additional information, see CRS Report RL33263, *The Wetlands Coverage of the Clean Water Act (CWA) Is Revisited by the Supreme Court Rapanos v. United States*, by Robert Meltz and Claudia Copeland.

---

authority from the Corps to EPA. The agencies are continuing to review permit applications for surface coal mining projects in Appalachia under existing rules, but not the vacated ECP.

In June 2010, the Army Corps suspended the use of a particular CWA general permit for surface coal mining activities in Appalachia. In February, the Corps reissued all of its CWA general permits, including one (nationwide permit 21) to replace the suspended permit with one containing more stringent CWA rules applicable to these coal mining operations.[87]

In November 2009, the Department of the Interior's Office of Surface Mining (OSM) issued an Advance Notice of Proposed Rulemaking (ANPR) describing options to revise a SMCRA rule that affects surface coal mining operations, called the stream buffer zone rule, which was promulgated in December 2008.[88] The Obama Administration identified the 2008 rule, which exempts so-called valley fills and other mining waste disposal activities from requirements to protect a 100-foot buffer zone around streams, for revision as part of the series of actions concerning surface coal mining in Appalachia. Since then, OSM officials have been working on developing a new rule and an accompanying draft environmental impact statement (EIS), with the goal of proposing a rule and a draft EIS later in 2012. The revised stream buffer zone rule, when promulgated, is expected to apply nationwide, not just in Appalachia. For additional information, contact Claudia Copeland (7-7227, ccopeland@crs.loc.gov).

Toxic Substances Control Act (TSCA)

36.-38. Lead: Renovation, Repair, and Painting Program Rules. EPA has revised a 2008 final rule implementing Section 402(c)(3) of the Toxic Substances Control Act (TSCA; enacted as the Residential Lead-Based Paint Hazard Reduction Act of 1992.) The rule aims to reduce human health hazards associated with exposure to lead-based paint. It established requirements for training and certifying workers and firms that remodel, repair, or paint homes or child-occupied public or commercial buildings likely to contain lead-based paint (generally built before 1978). Shortly after promulgation of the 2008 version of the rule, several petitions were filed challenging it. The U.S. Court of Appeals for the District of Columbia Circuit consolidated the petitions and, in August 2009, EPA signed a settlement agreement with the petitioners. The agreement set legal deadlines for a number of EPA rulemaking actions. One rule proposed May 6, 2010, addresses public and commercial buildings that are not child-occupied.[89] A final version of that rule is expected in 2015, according to the Unified Regulatory Agenda issued for fall 2011. A second rule, also proposed in May 2010, addressed the testing requirements after renovations are complete.[90] That rule was revised and promulgated July 15, 2011, effective October 4, 2011.[91] The third rule,

---

[87] For information see CRS Report 97-223, *The Army Corps of Engineers' Nationwide Permits Program Issues and Regulatory Developments*, by Claudia Copeland.

[88] U.S. Department of the Interior, Office of Surface Mining Reclamation and Enforcement, "Stream Buffer Zone and Related Rules; Advance notice of proposed rulemaking; notice of intent to prepare a supplemental environmental impact statement (SEIS)," 74 *Federal Register* 62664-62668, November 30, 2009.

[89] U.S. Environmental Protection Agency, "Lead; Renovation, Repair, and Painting Program for Public and Commercial Buildings; Proposed Rule," 75 *Federal Register* 24848-24862, May 6, 2010.

[90] U.S. Environmental Protection Agency, "Clearance and Clearance Testing Requirements for the Renovation, Repair, and Painting Program: Lead; Proposed Rule," 75 Federal Register 25038-25073, May 6, 2010.

[91] U.S. Environmental Protection Agency, "Lead: Clearance and Clearance Testing Requirements for the Renovation, Repair, and Painting Program," Final Rule, 76 *Federal Register* 47918-47946, July 15, 2011.

promulgated in May 2010, eliminated an opt-out provision that would have exempted a renovation firm from training and work practice requirements if certification were obtained from the property owner that no child under age 6 or pregnant woman resides in a facility and no children spend significant amounts of time there.[92] That rule also revises recordkeeping and disclosure provisions. EPA has estimated that this third rule would add $500 million to the cost of the 2008 renovation, repair, and painting program in the first year and $300 million per year starting with the second year. In 2010, Congress included a provision in P.L. 111-212, a supplemental appropriations act, which prohibited the use of "funds made available by this Act" to levy fines or to hold any person liable for work performed under the rule. However, P.L. 111-212 provided no funds to EPA for those purposes, so the provision had no effect on EPA's use of existing funds that had been appropriated in P.L. 111-88 to enforce the rule.[93] In June 2010, on its own initiative, EPA published a memorandum informing enforcement division directors in the regional offices that the Agency would not enforce certain requirements for certification of firms or for individual training until after October 1, 2010. However, individual renovators must have been enrolled in required training classes before that date and all must have completed required training prior to December 31, 2010, according to the memorandum. For additional information, contact Linda-Jo Schierow (7-7279, lschierow@crs.loc.gov)

Solid Waste (RCRA)

39. Coal Combustion Waste. In 2008, coal-fired power plants accounted for almost half of U.S. electric power, resulting in approximately 136 million tons of coal combustion waste (CCW). On December 22, 2008, national attention was turned to risks associated with managing CCW when a breach in a surface impoundment pond at the Tennessee Valley Authority's Kingston, TN, plant released 1.1 billion gallons of coal ash slurry, covering hundreds of acres and damaging or destroying homes and property. In addition to the risk of a sudden, catastrophic release such as that at Kingston, EPA has determined that CCW disposal in unlined landfills and surface impoundments presents substantial risks to human health and the environment from releases of toxic constituents (particularly arsenic and selenium) into surface and groundwater. To establish national standards intended to address risks associated with potential CCW mismanagement, on June 21, 2010, EPA proposed two regulatory options to manage the waste.[94] The first option would draw on EPA's existing authority to identify a waste as hazardous and regulate it under the waste management standards established under Subtitle C of the Resource Conservation and Recovery Act (RCRA). The second option would establish regulations applicable to CCW disposal units under RCRA's Subtitle D solid waste management requirements. Under Subtitle D, EPA does not have the authority to implement or enforce its proposed requirements. Instead, EPA would rely on states or citizen suits to enforce new standards. In its Regulatory Impact Analysis, EPA estimated the average annualized regulatory costs to be approximately $1.5 billion a year under the Subtitle C option or $587 million a year under the Subtitle D option, but there could be additional costs or benefits depending on how the rule affects the recycling of coal ash.

---

[92] U.S. Environmental Protection Agency, "Amendment to the Opt-out and Recordkeeping Provisions in the Renovation, Repair, and Painting Program: Lead; Final Rule," 75 Federal Register 24802-24819, May 6, 2010.

[93] Sven-Erik Kaiser, EPA Congressional Liaison, personal communication, Sept. 14, 2011.

[94] U.S. Environmental Protection Agency, "Hazardous and Solid Waste Management System; Identification and Listing of Special Wastes; Disposal of Coal Combustion Residuals From Electric Utilities," 75 *Federal Register* 35127-35264, June 21, 2010.

EPA has not projected a date to promulgate a final rule. However, on April 5, 2012, a coalition of environmental groups filed suit to compel EPA to finalize its proposed rulemaking.[95] For additional information, contact Linda Luther (7-6852, lluther@crs.loc.gov).

40. Identification of Non-Hazardous Materials That Are Solid Wastes When Burned. In conjunction with emission standards for boilers and solid waste incinerators discussed above in items 18, 19, and 20, in February 2011, EPA finalized regulations intended to clarify when certain materials burned as fuel in a combustion unit would be considered a "solid waste."[96] The definition of solid waste plays an important role in implementing the emission standards for both boilers and solid waste incinerators. The 2007 D.C. Circuit decision that vacated EPA's previous emission standards for boilers also vacated EPA's definition of terms under its "CISWI Definitions Rule."[97] The D.C. Circuit concluded that EPA erred in defining "commercial and industrial solid waste" to exclude solid waste that is burned at a facility in a combustion unit whose design provides for energy recovery or which operates with energy recovery. Instead, the D.C. Circuit stated that the Clean Air Act "requires any unit that combusts 'any solid waste material at all'—regardless of whether the material is being burned for energy recovery—to be regulated as a 'solid waste incineration unit.'"[98] The final rule addresses issues brought up by the D.C. Circuit and, in doing so, significantly narrows the current universe of non-hazardous secondary materials that could be burned in boilers.[99] EPA anticipates that boiler operators that burn materials newly-identified as a solid waste would switch to a non-waste fuel, rather than being subject to the more stringent emission standards applicable to solid waste incinerators (item 18 above). The final rule also addresses a host of concerns raised by various stakeholders during the public comment period for the proposed rule, including those of several Members of Congress. In particular, the final rule clarifies that the definition of solid waste would not affect current used oil recycling regulations (which allows burning used oil in space heaters, under certain conditions) and explicitly excludes from the definition of solid waste "scrap tires used in a combustion unit that are … managed under the oversight of established tire collection programs." EPA states that this regulatory action would not directly invoke any costs or benefits. Instead, any costs or benefits would be related to the Boiler MACT and CISWI Standards (see items 18, 19, and 20, above). On December 23, 2011, EPA proposed reconsideration of the final rule that would amend and clarify specific elements of the regulations (under 40 CFR Part 241). The proposed amendments were jointly proposed with EPA's reconsideration of the CISWI proposed rule (item 18, above). Although EPA originally anticipated that both proposed would be finalized in April 2012, it is unclear when the rule will be complete. For additional information, contact Linda Luther (7-6852, lluther@crs.loc.gov).

---

[95] Appalachian Voices et al. v. Lisa P. Jackson, Case No. 1:12-cv-00523 (D.D.C.), April 5, 2012.

[96] Environmental Protection Agency, Final Rule, "Identification of Non-Hazardous Secondary Materials That Are Solid Waste," 76 *Federal Register* 15455, March 21, 2011.

[97] Environmental Protection Agency, Final Rule, "Standards of Performance for New Stationary Sources and Emission Guidelines for Existing Sources: Commercial and Industrial Solid Waste Incineration Units," 70 *Federal Register* 55568, September 22, 2005.

[98] This and related court finding are discussed in the final rule at 76 *Federal Register* 15461.

[99] See EPA's web page "Identification of Non-Hazardous Materials That Are Solid Waste: Final Rulemaking" at http://www.epa.gov/epawaste/nonhaz/define/index.htm.

Table 2. Major or Controversial Rules Promulgated by EPA Since January 2009

Item No.	Statutory Authority	Rule	Status	Court or Legislative Requirement?	Affected Entities
1.	Clean Air Act	Greenhouse Gas (GHG) Reporting Rule	Promulgated October 30, 2009. Other categories of sources have subsequently been added, the latest on November 8, 2010. First data were released 1/11/12.	Required by FY2008 EPA appropriation (P.L. 110-161).	About 10,000 facilities in 31 categories were affected by the original rule. Eleven categories with about 3,000 more facilities were subsequently added.
2.	Clean Air Act	GHG Endangerment Finding	Promulgated December 15, 2009.	A determination was required by the Supreme Court decision in *Massachusetts v. EPA*, April 2, 2007.	Prerequisite to finalizing EPA's GHG emission standards for cars and light-duty trucks, promulgated April 1, 2010; these, in turn, triggered GHG permit requirements for stationary sources.
3.	Clean Air Act	Light Duty Motor Vehicle GHG Rule for Model Years 2012-2016	Promulgated May 7, 2010.	Required by Section 202 of the Clean Air Act once the agency found endangerment of pub ic health or welfare from GHG emissions.	New cars, minivans, SUVs, and ight trucks, beginning in model year 2012. EPA estimates the lifetime increased cost for 2012-2016 vehicles at $52 billion, with $240 bil ion in expected benefits.
4.	Clean Air Act	GHG Tailoring Rule	Promulgated June 3, 2010.	None	Limits to an estimated 1,600 the number of facilities required to obtain GHG emission permits over each of the years 2011-2013.
5.	Clean Air Act	PSD and Title V Permit Requirements for GHG Emissions	Effective January 2, 2011.	Required once the Light Duty Motor Vehicle Rule was promulgated.	App ies only to large stationary sources identified by the Tailoring Rule.

Item No.	Statutory Authority	Rule	Status	Court or Legislative Requirement?	Affected Entities
6.	Clean Air Act	Medium- and Heavy-Duty Vehicle GHG Rule	Promulgated September 15, 2011.	Fuel economy standards were required by Section 102 of EISA (P.L. 110-140). GHG standards were required once EPA finalized the endangerment finding, and were harmonized with the fuel economy proposal.	New trucks beginning in model year 2014. EPA estimates increased costs for 2014-2018 vehicles at $8.1 billion, with $57 bil ion in projected benefits.
8.	Clean Air Act	Expanded Renewable Fuel Standard (RFS2)	Promulgated March 26, 2010 for 2010; on December 21, 2010 for 2011; and on January 9, 2012 for 2012.	Decisions required by the Energy Independence and Security Act of 2007.	Petroleum refiners, biofuel producers.
9.	Clean Air Act	Ethanol Blend Wall Waiver	EPA granted a partial waiver for E15 use in 2007 and newer passenger cars and light trucks, November 4, 2010. On January 21, 2011, EPA announced that the waiver would be expanded to include MY2001-MY2006 vehicles.	The Energy Independence and Security Act of 2007 mandates increased use of renewable fuels. Unless EPA grants a Clean Air Act waiver to allow increased use of ethanol in gasoline, it will be difficult to meet this mandate.	Gasoline refiners and blenders, auto manufacturers, and manufacturers of engines for outdoor equipment of all types.
10.	Clean Air Act	National Ambient Air Quality Standard for Ozone	Proposed January 19, 2010; withdrawn September 2, 2011.	In response to petitions for review, EPA agreed to reconsider the ozone NAAQS promulgated in March 2008. Court challenge to the 2008 standards (*Mississippi v. EPA*) was stayed pending the reconsideration, but is now proceeding.	Recent ozone levels in the vast majority of the 675 counties with monitors would have violated the proposed standard; implementation of the proposed standard could have led to widespread new emission controls at a projected cost of $19 bil ion to $90 bil ion annually in 2020, with comparable levels of benefits, according to EPA.

Item No.	Statutory Authority	Rule	Status	Court or Legislative Requirement?	Affected Entities
12.	Clean Air Act	National Ambient Air Quality Standard for Sulfur Dioxide (SO₂)	Promulgated June 22, 2010.	D.C. Circuit remanded the SO₂ standard to EPA in 1998; EPA acted under a consent decree.	Principal effects would be to require additional controls on coal-fired electric power plants; EPA estimates costs at $1.8 billion to $6.8 billion annually, with benefits 5-6 times that amount.
13.	Clean Air Act	Cross-State Air Pollution Rule	Promulgated August 8, 2011. Implementation was stayed by the D.C. Circuit Court of Appeals, December 30, 2011. Oral argument occurred April 13, 2012.	D.C. Circuit remanded the rule to EPA in 2008.	Affects electric power plants in 28 eastern states; sets up cap-and-trade programs for SO₂ and NOx, at a projected annual cost of $2.4 billion, with benefits of $120 billion to $280 billion annually, according to EPA.
14.	Clean Air Act	Mercury and Air Toxics Standards / MACT for Electric Generating Units ("Utility MACT")	EPA promulgated the standards February 16, 2012.	Clean Air Mercury Rule was vacated and remanded to EPA in February 2008. EPA, under a consent decree, agreed to promulgate MACT standards by November 16, 2011.	Coal-fired electric generating units, which generate about 45% of the nation's electricity. EPA estimates annual cost at $9.6 billion, with benefits of $37 billion to $90 billion annually.
19.	Clean Air Act	Portland Cement Manufacturing MACT and NSPS	Promulgated September 9, 2010.	Earlier standards, promulgated in 1999, were remanded to the agency by the D.C. Circuit Court of Appeals. EPA promulgated a replacement in 2006, but subsequently agreed to reconsider the replacement rules.	Portland cement manufacturing industry. About 158 cement kilns operating at nearly 100 locations are affected by the rules.

Item No.	Statutory Authority	Rule	Status	Court or Legislative Requirement?	Affected Entities
20.	Clean Air Act	RICE Rule for Stationary Diesel Engines	Promulgated March 3, 2010.	The standards respond in part to a December 2008 DC. Circuit Court of Appeals ruling that EPA's air toxics standards must address emissions during all phases of operation including periods of startup, shutdown, and malfunction. The schedule for completing this rule was estab ished by a consent decree.	900,000 engines used as backup generators or to power compressors and pumps by industrial, agricultural, or oil and gas industry sources.
21.	Clean Air Act	RICE Rule for Stationary Spark-Ignition Engines	Promulgated August 20, 2010.	Same as Item 20.	330,000 engines used as backup generators or to power compressors and pumps by industrial, agricultural, or oil and gas industry sources.
22.	Clean Air Act	Emission Standards for New Marine (C3) Engines	Promulgated April 30, 2010.	None, but EPA had committed to promulgate the standards when issuing earlier standards in 2003.	The standards, which affect new marine engines for ocean-going ships beginning in 2011, were generally supported by the shipping industry,
23.	Clean Air Act	Emission Control Areas for Ocean-Going Ships	International Maritime Organization gave final approval to EPA's proposal in March 2010.	None	The measure, which is supported by the maritime industry, will require use of low sulfur fuels within 200 nautical miles of most of the U.S. coast.
24.	Clean Air Act	Oil and Natural Gas Air Pollution Standards	Promulgated April 17, 2012	EPA acted under a consent agreement signed in February 2010 to revise existing NSPS and hazardous pollutant rules.	About 11,000 new natural gas wells will be affected annually. The standards are the first national air emission standards for hydraulically fractured wells.

Item No.	Statutory Authority	Rule	Status	Court or Legislative Requirement?	Affected Entities
27.	Clean Water Act	Pesticide Application General Permit	EPA issued a final permit on October 31, 2011.	2009 federal court ruling invalidated a 2006 EPA rule.	Estimated universe of affected activities is approximately 5.6 million applications annually, performed by 365,000 applicators.
28.	Clean Water Act	Florida Nutrient Water Quality Standards	EPA promulgated numeric nutrient standards for Florida inland waters on December 5, 2010. Standards for other Florida waters are to be issued by November 2012.	2009 federal consent decree establishing a schedule for EPA to issue numeric nutrient standards.	Would likely affect a broad array of industrial and municipal dischargers and possibly sources of nonpoint pollution (e.g., agricultural lands).
29.	Clean Water Act	Chesapeake Bay TMDL	EPA finalized a TMDL on December 29, 2010. Bay jurisdictions are developing Watershed Implementation Plans.	Consent decrees required EPA to develop a TMDL by May 1, 2011.	Potentially could require additional pollution control by many point and nonpoint sources throughout the Chesapeake Bay watershed.
33.	Clean Water Act	SPCC Revisions, including Compliance Date Extension for Farms and Exemption for Milk Storage	Final rule extending compliance date to May 10, 2013, was promulgated November 22, 2011. Final rule for milk storage exemption was promulgated April 18, 2011.	None	Farms subject to SPCC provisions and applicable facilities that store oil, which includes milk.

Source: Compiled by CRS.

Table 3. Major Rules Under Development at EPA

Item No.	Statutory Authority	Rule	Status	Court or Legislative Requirement?	Affected Entities
3.	Clean Air Act	Light Duty Motor Vehicle GHG Rule for Model Years 2017-2025	Proposed, December 1, 2011.	Proposal is based on the Supreme Court decision in *Massachusetts v. EPA*, April 2, 2007, and the subsequent Endangerment Finding (see Item 2).	New cars, minivans, SUVs, and ight trucks, beginning in model year 2017. EPA estimates the cost of the proposed standards for 2017-2025 model vehicles at $140 billion, with benefits of $561 billion.
7.	Clean Air Act	NSPS to Control GHG Emissions from Petroleum Refineries	On December 23, 2010, EPA released the text of a settlement agreement with 11 states, two municipalities, and three environmental groups, under which it agreed to propose the NSPS by December 10, 2011, and take final action on the proposal by November 10, 2012. As of April 2012, the standards had not been proposed.	EPA has been sued by numerous parties for its failure to issue NSPS for GHG emissions from refineries (*American Petroleum Institute v. EPA*). Section 111(b) of the Clean Air Act requires NSPS for a category of sources if it "causes, or contributes significantly to air pollution which may reasonably be anticipated to endanger public health or welfare."	Petroleum refineries, which EPA concludes are the second-largest direct stationary source of GHGs in the United States.
11.	Clean Air Act	National Ambient Air Quality Standard for Particulate Matter (PM), including "farm dust"	Proposal expected in June 2012.	D.C. Circuit remanded the 2006 fine particulate ($PM_{2.5}$) standards to EPA in February 2009. Clean Air Act required review by October 2011.	PM standards affect a wide range of sources because they address all kinds of particles and aerosols in the atmosphere.

Item No.	Statutory Authority	Rule	Status	Court or Legislative Requirement?	Affected Entities
15.	Clean Air Act	NSPS to Control GHG Emissions from Electric Generating Units	EPA proposed standards March 27, 2012. Under a settlement agreement with 11 states and other parties, EPA agreed to take final action on the proposal by May 26, 2012, a date that now appears unlikely.	EPA was sued by numerous parties for its failure to issue NSPS for GHG emissions from power plants (*State of New York v. EPA*). Section 111(b) of the Clean Air Act requires NSPS for a category of sources if it "causes, or contributes significantly to air pollution which may reasonably be anticipated to endanger public health or welfare." EPA has already concluded that GHGs are such air pollution. Electric generating units account for one-third of all U.S. GHG emissions.	Primarily coal-fired electric generating units, which generate about 45% of the nation's electricity.
16.	Clean Air Act	MACT to Control Air Toxics from Boilers ("Boiler MACT")	Finalized February 21, 2011, The agency began reconsideration of elements of the rule the same day. Revisions were proposed December 23, 2011.	D.C. Circuit vacated the rule in 2007. D.C. District Court set deadline for promulgation.	Would affect a broad array of industrial, commercial, and institutional facilities. EPA estimates annual cost at $1.5 billion, with annual benefits of $27 billion to $67 billion.
17.	Clean Air Act	Area Source Standards for Boilers	Finalized February 21, 2011. The agency began reconsideration of elements of the rule the same day. Revisions were proposed December 23, 2011.	D.C. Circuit vacated the boiler and related incinerator rules in 2007.	Boilers at thousands of smaller commercial, industrial, and institutional facilities.

Item No.	Statutory Authority	Rule	Status	Court or Legislative Requirement?	Affected Entities
18.	Clean Air Act	CISWI Incinerator Standards	Fina ized February 21, 2011, (along with RCRA rules to identify non-hazardous materials that are so id wastes when burned—see item 40). The agency began reconsideration of elements of the rule the same day, and revisions were proposed December 23, 2011.	D.C. Circuit vacated the rule in 2007.	88 boilers that qualify as incinerators because they burn so id waste.
25.	Clean Air Act	Tier 3 Motor Vehicle Emission and Fuel Standards	EPA expects to propose a rule in July 2012.	None	New car and ight truck manufacturers; petroleum refiners.
26.	Clean Water Act	Construction Site Effluent Limitation Guidelines	Rule was promulgated December 1, 2009. A portion of the rule has been stayed for reconsideration. EPA expects to issue a final rule by November 19, 2012.	Federal court ordered EPA to issue the final rule by December 1, 2009.	Affects about 82,000 firms involved in residential, commercial, highways, street, and bridge construction.
30.	Clean Water Act	"Post-Construction" Stormwater Rule	EPA expects to propose a rule in April 2012.	May 2012 consent decree.	Unknown at this time.
31.	Clean Water Act	Revised Cooling Water Intake Rule	EPA proposed regulations March 28, 2011. Final rule is due by July 27, 2012.	EPA rules issued in 2004 were remanded by order of a federal court.	Proposal app ies to approximately 1,150 existing power plants and certain other manufacturing facilities.
32.	Clean Water Act	Revised Steam Electric Effluent Guidelines	A proposed rule is due by July 23, 2012.	November 2010 consent decree requires EPA to propose revised rules by July 2012 and promulgate final rule by January 2014.	Proposal will apply to existing and new steam electric power plants.
34.	Clean Water Act	'Waters of the United States' Guidance	Revised guidance proposed April 27, 2011.	None	Potentially affects a wide range of entities and activities subject to CWA requirements, including permits.

Item No.	Statutory Authority	Rule	Status	Court or Legislative Requirement?	Affected Entities
35.	Clean Water Act and Surface Mining Control and Reclamation Act	Mountaintop Mining in Appalachia	Various short-term and long-term actions are underway by EPA and other agencies to strengthen environmental reviews and revise regulations.	None	Surface coal mining operations in the Appalachian region.
36-38.	Toxic Substances Control Act	Lead Renovation, Repair, and Painting	Final rule eliminating the opt-out provision was promulgated May 6, 2010. Final rule regarding clearance testing requirements was promulgated July 15, 2011. A rule for work in pub ic and commercial buildings was proposed May 6, 2010, and is expected to be finalized in 2015.	August 2009 settlement agreement set numerous dead ines for revisions of a 2008 lead rule.	Workers and firms that remodel, repair, or paint homes and some commercial buildings.
39.	Resource Conservation and Recovery Act (RCRA)	Coal Combustion Waste	Proposed June 21, 2010.	None	Coal-fired electric power plants.
40.	Resource Conservation and Recovery Act (RCRA)	Identification of Non-Hazardous Materials That Are Solid Wastes When Burned	Fina ized February 21, 2011 (along with CAA boiler MACT and area source rules and CISWI standards—see items 16-18). The agency began a reconsideration of elements of the rule the same day. Revisions were proposed December 23, 2011.	In 2007 D.C. Circuit vacated the CISWI definitions rule in a decision that also addressed CISWI and boiler MACT standards.	Combustion units that burn non-hazardous secondary materials.

Source: Compiled by CRS.

Author Contact Information

James E. McCarthy
Specialist in Environmental Policy
jmccarthy@crs.loc.gov, 7-7225

Claudia Copeland
Specialist in Resources and Environmental Policy
ccopeland@crs.loc.gov, 7-7227

Key Policy and Legal Staff

Other CRS analysts, listed below, contributed to this report.

Area of Expertise	Name	Phone	E-mail
Regulatory reform	Maeve Carey	7-7775	mcarey@crs.loc.gov
Clean Water Act	Claudia Copeland	7-7227	ccopeland@crs.loc.gov
Clean Air Act, oil and natural gas	Rick Lattanzio	7-1754	rlattanzio@crs.loc.gov
Solid Waste	Linda Luther	7-6852	lluther@crs.loc.gov
Clean Air Act	Jim McCarthy	7-7225	jmccarthy@crs.loc.gov
Environmental law	Rob Meltz	7-7891	rmeltz@crs.loc.gov
Oil Spill Prevention	Jonathan Ramseur	7-7919	jramseur@crs.loc.gov
Toxic Substances Control Act	Linda-Jo Schierow	7-7279	lschierow@crs.loc.gov
Safe Drinking Water Act	Mary Tiemann	7-5937	mtiemann@crs.loc.gov
Clean Air Act, mobile sources, CAFE	Brent Yacobucci	7-9662	byacobucci@crs.loc.gov